J. FINN

Emotional Intelligence Insights for Self Mastery

Mindfulness Tips to Cultivate a Calm Mind, Break Free from Limiting Beliefs, & Embrace Your True Power

Copyright © 2025 by J. Finn

All rights reserved. No part of this publication may be reproduced, stored or transmitted in any form or by any means, electronic, mechanical, photocopying, recording, scanning, or otherwise without written permission from the publisher. It is illegal to copy this book, post it to a website, or distribute it by any other means without permission.

J. Finn is not a certified counselor or a financial advisor and is not suggesting you take any actions whatsoever based on what you read in this book. You must do your own due diligence. Only you are responsible for your actions and your life.

First edition

ISBN (paperback): 979-8-9923783-0-6
ISBN (hardcover): 979-8-9923783-1-3

Advisor: The Great Beings Within
Cover art by 99designs.com

This book was professionally typeset on Reedsy.
Find out more at reedsy.com

Dedicated to the ones who lit the way before.
All the gratitude goes to you.

Contents

Foreword		ii
Preface		iv
1	Introduction	1
2	The Way	12
3	Inner Freedom	25
4	Fear	38
5	True Love	49
6	Heartbreak	66
7	Failure	79
8	Death	88
9	Manipulation	96
10	Temptation	103
11	Money	112
12	Time	123
13	The Matrix	136
14	Pervading Stillness	145
15	Manifestation	152
16	Inner Truth	164
17	Glossary	185
18	Thank You!	188

FREE BONUS + ZOOM MEETING ACCESS

arkofarion.com/freebonus

ENTER YOUR EMAIL TO RECEIVE YOUR FREE BONUSES & THE ZOOM LINK!

JOIN US LIVE ON ZOOM
SUNDAYS @ 10:00 AM CENTRAL TIME

Zoom is intended to complement our Self Love Workbook

Bring your coffee or morning beverage of choice! This is a low-key Sunday event, but please be prepared to have your video ON otherwise there will be no community vibe.

What to bring:
- Any questions you have about the program
- Anything you want to share about your progress and/or obstacles you're experiencing
- Any sharable insights you discover throughout each week

What to expect:
- A 30-60 minute casual event
- Only share if you want to!
- We will do 1 or 2 short meditations
- We will fill out the Sunday morning section together
- If someone feels the need to be heard or supported, we are here to hold space for that. BUT I am not a professional counselor, and the group is not here to disrespect anyone present or not present.

This is sacred space, a safe place to be seen, to open & share from the Heart Center, where we are each learning to confidently captain our ships, & repair them as necessary!

We are here to witness each other's self awareness journey. Please no offering advice to anyone while in our live Zoom calls UNLESS of course someone explicitly asks for feedback or thoughts from the group.

Preface

This book is designed to be a key to your heart, a key out of your mind—a key to restart. The journey you'll embark on, if you choose this noble quest, will not only enhance your life, but will alter your current perspectives.

You will learn to see with more clarity. Confidence will come naturally. You will clear the path to manifesting greatness effortlessly.

The more energy you dedicate to this path, the more clearly you will comprehend your unique factor, which is the ultimate key to monetary abundance, if that is your goal. Just remember: the joy is in the journey, not in your bank account number.

You will learn to forgive yourself, love and respect yourself, become a great leader of yourself, strengthen your boundaries with others, and take back your power. You will see how emotions and colorful life events are tools you can use to level-up your self-awareness.

If you need a self-esteem boost, you've come to the right place, especially if you've ever dealt with fear, failure, or heartbreak. You will learn how to use time more effectively and focus your precious attention (which really is the most valuable commodity on this planet).

If you feel you're caught in the rat race and want to find a way out, you may choose this admirable mission to regain your inner throne and remember your royal, divine heritage.

Uncover who you really are.

In the chapters that follow, we cover topics that influence our lives in both positive and negative ways, such as love, money, manipulation, and temptation. There are times in life we might find ourselves stagnating, and at other times we may choose an unhealthy path. All of life's events have the potential to cause a roller coaster of thoughts and emotions, affecting your way of living and how much you're able to express yourself.

With that in mind, our goal is to shake up your thought patterns, to more easily identify (and then later on, restructure) the parts of your day-to-day life that are not serving your highest power, to then make space for your true desires to come forward. We hope with these writings you begin identifying the clutter that surrounds you, so you may clear it away, recognize your true purpose, and make every single one of your days better than before.

This book is best read a little at a time, as some ideas require time to be processed. Some require repetition to help re-program your neural networks into a cleaner patterning that aligns with your Inner Truth—the real you.

The general tone throughout these writings is peaceful, but you will find some parts have a jolting, harsh vibe. This is intended to draw you out of the hypnotic state many of us have fallen into in our civilized, distracted, technological lives.

We are all on our own paths of infinite blossoming and expansion. The further we go, the steeper the learning curve seems to become, so it is our mission to provide a more illuminated on-ramp—or at least to offer a light wherever someone may be starting from.

I hope that by reading this book, with this shift in perspective, you will gain something of value to apply to your everyday life.

Notes from The Great Beings Within

As time rolls on and becomes stranger and stranger, you may question your purpose for being here. You might ask yourself, "What's the point?" "Does any of this matter?" "No really, why am I here??" This book provides the answer. There is a better way—one that was intended all along. The untrained brain is responsible for much of what has occurred here – the complexities, confusion, mortality rates, etc... But there are no enemies, no one to blame—just your own unclear vision.

The key out of this mess is not in your mind. The key or access point to your natural clarity and peaceful, centered state is in your heart. The answers to all the questions you've ever asked or pondered over can all be answered right now. The answers lie within. All you must do is sit down alone, quiet the mind, be still, and listen. It is as simple as that.

This book is a guide on how to become a *master* of your mind (is the brain really the untrained *beast* the world has spoken of all this time?). The chapters that follow will teach you how to lead yourself (and others) into a new golden era of peace and harmony, and how to be the influential leader you are destined to be.

By following the straightforward directions on how to find and follow your unique path, you can achieve the fulfillment, happiness, and love each person born onto this planet desires. You deserve to experience greatness and to see your wildest dreams coming true.

The contents of this book include basic principles followed by many enlightened Beings for achieving higher levels of understanding about Truth and reality—enlightenment. The same destiny awaits you, if you so choose.

1

Introduction

There once was a time, in a land far away, when a prophecy was made, in which Source would have Its day, and be seen for what It is and was. No second guesses, no regrets, just simply *be-cause*. It chose Earth for this great and noble cause—to express Itself into physical form and to enjoy abundance in every way It could ever want. Source chose the human body to make this dream a reality, so that It could express infinite uniqueness and diversity much more easily.

Each human being carries with them a special gift inside, that which we will call the "unique factor." This factor allows everyone to build the world, not as competitors, but as team players, so that there is no need for thoughts of scarcity or competition. Each human is born with the ability to draw from an infinite pool of inspiration—the Source of everything that has ever been created.

Human beings were given a brain and a heart as their greatest tools of manifestation for this infinite expression. Source intended to flow through each person's heart with inspired, flawless creativity, which would then be conceptualized and made manifest by thoughts from the brain, and put into the world using the body. Everything was going according to plan… until the brain-heart connection was gradually forgotten.…

The brain, wired to handle physical-world matters, has wrapped you up in this physical life, into this game of "live or die." The untrained brain clings to and identifies with many silly distractions in the physical realm — the great web or matrix as some call it. Your real Self—the soul, the Great Observer — sees this fault. There is a way to view your life with clear eyes, so that you become the *observer* of the external world while you manifest your greatest desires into the physical, which are more like trophies or beautiful cherries atop the greatest accomplishments you achieve *within* yourself first — the masterpiece dessert.

Your soul sprouted into form with unmatched grace and perfection. Even if you've "been through the wringer" through childhood and into adulthood, you can still access this pure space of creativity and centeredness within. But, to safely become a "deep diver" of your soul requires patience, persistence, and practice. Most people, lacking self-awareness or bombarded with their fears, have become surface dwellers, only seeking surface-level experiences, shallow connections with others, and external validation. They may want more, but they may not see The Way.

This ability to reach inside and access your Source energy is where true, fulfilling greatness derives, and once you learn to access it with ease, eliminating all your past resistance and future worries, you will finally be living in the present moment, completely fulfilled and dis-ease-free… Then, perhaps, your body will no longer age, or at the very least, you will enjoy abundance in all its desirable forms. Then you may teach.

Keep in mind, to achieve great accomplishments such as immortality or instant manifestation involves a path of exceptional transformation which may feel like death from time to time. There are times you will think you have damaged yourself, especially if you do not learn the difference between *you* and the baggage you insist upon carrying along with you.

To traverse this path entails letting go of *everything* that is holding you back, including things (and people) you hang on to simply as security blankets. If you hold on to past regrets, negative beliefs about yourself, bad relationships, bad habits, mistakes, or grudges, you place a heavy burden on your soul and heart, which effectively cut you off from your birthright access to the timeless present moment. If left to fester and rot, such burdens can develop into life-threatening illness. It is strange, is it not, how illness and severe dis-ease are commonplace among such civilized people… Or perhaps something is amiss…. What is it? Are we diseased, or are we simply seeing out of focus?

The Daily Work - How to Clear the Mind and Focus

Within these pages, we discuss the practices of "going within" and the "Daily Work," for these are the secrets to gaining answers to all the questions you have ever asked. This Daily Work quiets the mind over time and helps you focus on your real purpose. On the energetic level, it cleans your body's frequency so that you can access a truly centered state, which is where your Source of power and creativity exists (as well as love and forgiveness).

Once you clear the weeds so-to-speak and are able to sit closer to your center, you will begin to see the purpose of all emotions that arise within you, without being swept into the hurricane of old thought and reactionary patterns. Then you may be in a position to learn from them, and finally release those that no longer serve you. Once you "lighten up" ie. drop that baggage, and start focusing on what it is you actually want, your daily life will become your ideal in less time than you might think is possible.

Two major components make up the Daily Work: solo meditation and contemplation time, and daily life integration of Universal Law. As you bring these core foundational practices into your day-to-day reality, you will more easily identify and clear away the clutter you've accumulated in your mind, in your home, in your life, and even in your body over the years. You will be able to focus with more certainty so that you can achieve your most exciting goals in a leisurely, enjoyable fashion.

Component 1: Meditation and Contemplation

One part of the Daily Work is solo meditation and contemplation. For many people (at least in the beginning), meditation may feel like a laborious, boring, unenjoyable task. Sitting "without thinking" is challenging, so most do not even attempt it, and instead drown out their internal noise with more noise.

Achieving this "no thought" state is not really the goal we're after here (at least not at this stage of the game). Rather, the goal is to hone your focus—to rein in your point of awareness. To do this at the start, it is important to distract the thinking mind with a repetitive activity or monotonous sound. You may try the many excellent guided meditations online if you want to focus on something such as healing the physical body or a relationship pattern.

We'd like to first find out what your inner self—the pure, untainted You—will reveal using classic shamanic drumming with a simple animal hide drum (recordings of which can be found online for free, or shamanism.org has mp3s for a few dollars). You can use other types of audio, but a consistent, fast-paced tone or beat without vocals is best.

- Sit in a quiet room, put headphones on, close your eyes, and play the fifteen-minute Michael Harner "Shamanic Drumming" track on YouTube.[1]
- Some practitioners suggest picturing a favorite, relaxing place in nature. You may also focus on a problem you are experiencing, a question you would like an answer to, or part of the body that is in pain. Or just focus on your breathing.
- As you relax and continue focusing on your topic of choice, you may enter a dream state, but you will be conscious of it. The best thing you can do is continue breathing, relaxing, and allow it to play *without* controlling it. Ask a question if you have one, and then wait for an answer to become clear.
- There are additional steps to this process if you feel called to take this journeying technique further. Shamanism.org is one of the best resources available.

---

[1] Michael Harner, "Michael Harner: Shamanic journey—15 minutes solo drumming," YouTube (Foundation for Shamanic Studies, June 16, 2015). https://www.youtube.com/watch?v=MmQ1H4wU0zs.

Do not be discouraged if nothing seems to happen the first few times you try this. The simple practice of relaxing and calming the thinking mind is important, both for your overall health and for achieving success on this inward path.

Integrating contemplation time into your evening routine will also be life-changing - either with eyes closed, with a notebook, or in front of a fire. Screen time has essentially taken up most of the evening time, but if you desire *more* in this life, the evenings must be used to process your days, to evaluate the progress you've made, and what you will do tomorrow to continue moving forward with your soul mission, whatever that may be.

Meditation is for relaxing. Contemplation is for processing, for example, the emotions we may not have had an opportunity to fully express or give space to during our hectic day. Building these habits is just one step closer to the level of self-care necessary to access a truly centered state - to experience that natural state of peace you rightfully deserve. You must take care of yourself, or you will rot from the inside out. If you do not first learn *how* to take care of yourself, and then dedicate time to do it, the show cannot go on.

Do your best not to consider building these habits as "self-discipline," for, your inner child will rebel instantly at the thought of being disciplined! Think of it as dedication - to yourself, to your greater purpose and soul mission, to you feeling proud of yourself when you wake up every day. When you care this deeply about yourself and your life, it will be reflected in your relationships, your emotional stability, and your access to the abundance of anything you want.

If you muster the ambition to make it this far, you have surpassed ninety-five percent of the masses. Most people will talk the big talk about "doing things differently next year" and then sit on the couch after work watching TV, or staring at a screen until they're too tired to think about goals or dreams. Excuses, excuses!

Component 2: Universal Law

The following fundamental principles of life, or "Universal Law", are designed to guide you toward greater self-awareness, so that you can clean up your energy field, strengthen your boundaries, build healthier relationships (you will see *every* interaction as fertile bonding ground), and ideally flow abundance in all areas of life you deem enjoyable.

Many of the following ideas sound nice on the surface. By spending real time to contemplate them so that they interact with and alter the root of your programmed thoughts about reality, only then will you make actual progress incorporating them into daily life. Feel free to take each one into a 10-minute closed-eye or fireside contemplation session. Then you will, ideally, walk about in your waking reality as though they were built into your DNA, as part of who you are.... though you might come to realize, they already are.

- Do unto others as you would have them do unto you.
- Do unto yourself as you would have others do unto you.
- Behave with kindness, dignity, and honor.
- Have respect for yourself and all others.
- Show courage when others are fearful, especially when fear is expected.
- Show compassion for all, especially in moments of another's weakness or in the revelation of heinous crimes

against humanity.
- Be noble when nothing is asked of you.
- Have mercy on the weak, but do not contribute to their downfall in life.
- Avoid rash decisions and substances which may cause rash behavior.
- Treat others as royalty, for this is also your own true nature.
- Regret nothing, but move forward with precision and certainty.
- Cherish this present moment, for it is your last, and ought to be your best.
- Understand that you are perfect as you are *now*.
- Find the answers you seek from within, for the only pure, untainted wisdom you will ever know resides within your core.
- Treat all of physical reality as you would your child or work of art, because life itself is the purest art form in the physical reality you call home.

You are the master of your reality. It is your prime responsibility to be pleased, fulfilled, and happy. Create the greatest treasures Earth has ever seen by going within and listening to the small voice until it becomes loud and clear. It is an honor to develop this skill and to go on this ancient journey. You will not be disappointed.

In any land where children develop the building blocks of morality, inner strength, and overall depth of character, dishonor does not exist. Communities that provide the proper environment to teach these things do not have a shortage of powerful leaders. Such communities are family-oriented, deeply aware of their roots, live in simplicity, close to the land, and in the moment. These types of great communities are dwindling in number, as this way of living fades and is perceived as an outdated, low-tech, scarcity-lifestyle. Only those who are old enough to have lived through widespread, nationwide catastrophe know the benefit of counting your blessings, and what it takes to build a strong character. Guide one child by these fundamental principles of life, and you will benefit an entire generation of humanity.

Whence This Information Derives

The Inner Well of Truth and Understanding lies within every Being born onto this planet, and is the original source of wisdom found in this book. This Well holds the real, pure innocence of All That Is, and anyone who desires to Know the Truth can access it. No one may take this Knowing away from you, though they may attempt to distract you in the external world from time to time (ie. enter-tain-ment). But, if you desire to remain on this planet for all of eternity in the Garden, where you were born, you must remember how to access your Source. You must learn how to focus on your purpose.

Life is everlasting in the present moment. When you tap back into it and allow your Source to flow through you, you will bear witness to the pureness of Truth which will pour forth, and become what some call the holy vessel. Please make no mistake - we are not here to push religion upon you. What we might say is that ancient spiritual texts touch on this process, but perhaps we have not yet realized the *how* of what is called "enlightenment". You do not need knowledge in the brain to experience this, or to express yourself in profound ways. In fact, the overuse of the brain is what has imprisoned the human population into this great game of *forgetting...* Who are you?

All you must do is release what no longer serves you to unlock your access point to unlimited Source power. That is the goal of this whole earthly experience: to light up the dark with your awareness. You cannot go wrong, but you can create resistance by hanging onto unnecessary baggage, which is the cause of pain and undesirable circumstances. As you find the way back Home to this crystal clear, centered frequency, you will see your resistance points as separate from you, and it will be quite simple to let them go and accept beneficial life changes. No need to rush this process.

The contents of this book are a cherished sampling from the Well, recorded by one Being so that others may grasp and digest these practices to find Truth for themselves. As a reader of these words, we hope you will gather something of value to begin or continue your own inner search.

Find your way, and may it be well lit.

With Love,
 The Great Beings Within

Contemplations

- What grudges are you holding on to?
- What life situations or habits do you feel embarrassed of, or give yourself a hard time about?
- What mistakes from your past have you not yet forgiven yourself for?
- What are two judgments you often make about someone

else? About yourself? How can you let these go?

2

The Way

In the beginning, Source created Human Beings and the Inner Work, so that these Beings would have something to strive toward in order to attain a sense of betterment and achievement. In this process of achieving greater levels of self-awareness and inward growth, each Being would continue on in his or her thought processes and inner exploration until they came to understand themselves and how to access their Source. This continuous achievement would be considered enlightenment on the physical plane, to experience an individualized form, while at the same time gaining glimpses of the One Entity, ideally creating a balance between both.

That was the general concept of the inception of life on this plane of existence—to be beacons of light upon this planet of darkness. But as the brain continues to create complexity in its thought forms, some Beings (perhaps *many* Beings) get lost on the way to enlightenment. There is a common mis-routing of focusing power occurring, which causes many to become trapped in the complexities of their external lives. They focus exclusively on outer world minutiae, fritter away time, and develop their minds in ways that do not resonate with Truth, but instead keep them preoccupied and tied to this man-made grid, this unnatural system—this artificial matrix.

Examples include engaging in gossip, drama, other forms of enter-tain-ment like screen time, social media, gambling, and other addictive behaviors, or working at jobs that are not satisfying and only pay the bills. These people see no better way to go and continue to cloud their vision more and more— a vicious cycle of the worst kind. But we all have the power to realize this simple mistake and pivot onto a path of deep fulfillment and elegance, where we can find contentment and access to our ultimate power source. This Path, also known as The Way, leads to the Kingdom Within — the Garden of Life.

The Way has been described by many as a gateway to Truth itself, as a method for living the perfect life, day in and day out. Each person is designed to traverse The Way in their own unique way (provided a few guidelines are remembered and taken to heart, for obvious moral and just purposes).

The Moral Compass

You must have your moral compass close to you at all times, for it is equivalent to your passport in the unseen realms. If you do not have it, or if it is not well-developed, you are not ready for this phase of development. If you do decide to step up to the plate, willing to display your moral compass proudly, then let the games begin!

The Universe is designed with frequencies which support peace, harmony, and acceptance. If you choose to step forth onto this path of power, you must prepare your body and mind to be cleared of all baggage and filth, so that the moral compass is free to align itself, as it naturally will, with these pure divine energies.

The beginning of the path can be painful if you are not willing to let go of what no longer serves you (ego death). This requires releasing false beliefs about yourself and all limiting ideas of what you *think* you deserve, including love and money.

Do not feel you're alone in this journey. The teachers appear when the student is ready to fine-tune their moral compass and carry it with them daily so they may advance on The Path with ease. This fine-tuning is a daily practice, requiring dedication, and requiring that the student honor the Self, first and foremost, with great awareness of what a distraction looks like, and what a leaky boundary feels like, for example. You cannot fathom the excitement and greatness that will unfold in your life when you commit to this Path. So, let your inner guidance lead you, and bear witness to the perfection that unfolds before you.

To conquer the world, nurture your soul. Treat others with courtesy and respect, and you will travel well through this life. Behave as if nothing in life is as you *think* it is. In other words, make no ego-derived assumptions. Instead, understand that all of life's experiences are there for you to realize Truth.

Forgiving Yourself

Self-forgiveness is a critical component of this Path. If you cannot love yourself and see your life's experiences for what they are—lessons to increase your self-awareness—you will be trapped in misery, and in some cases, a victim mentality. You will stagnate, manifest diseases, and grow deep wrinkles on the face. *Or* you can love yourself, accept the hard lessons you've learned, and move on!

Out of Pain & Suffering Comes Truth

Once you open yourself to the Truth, you will never, and can never, go back without experiencing an even greater degree of excruciating pain. The pain is there to show you the boundaries of your Reality. It is like a wall to show you that this painful way is not the way toward your highest good — this is not the way to go to achieve your true greatness.

Sometimes the inner blindness is so intense that we (or we watch someone else) examine every square inch of these walls of pain and suffering. Sometimes this is what is needed to achieve some level of certainty. Finally when we've spent years feeling around in the darkness of the same types of relationships and experiencing the same types of trauma responses that echo from childhood, we finally Know (at the deepest level) that it's time to move on in another direction. The better direction suddenly, or gradually, becomes perfectly clear. This is a permanently learned lesson, so really there is nothing to feel ashamed of by learning the way *you* need to.

The Sacred Self Awareness Journey

You do not need to judge yourself or another for their determination to dig so deeply into such a resistant pattern, for we are all explorers of this energetic realm. We all must explore within our unique self awareness journey. If someone feels the need to dig a little deeper into that wall, who knows, there might be some treasure there, a priceless insight, that could have the power to light up the entirety of that particular wall or trauma pattern, and not just for that one person. The treasure they mine or clarity they achieve could be the light switch for the entire population.

Perhaps we could consider these energetic patterns equivalent to parasites. They hold us outside of our center, in a scattered sort of dirty frequency, they feed upon our energy, taking away precious focusing power, taking us away from the present moment constantly. But once we become aware of these "parasites", we take back our power and gain valuable footing back in the direction we want our lives to go, and not in the direction our emotional parasitic tornadoes push us toward.

Oath of Forgiveness

The Oath of Forgiveness is meant to be a way of life, a promise that must be renewed daily. It is a promise to yourself that you will live out your time with grace, gratitude, and respect for yourself and all others. Most people choose to live under heavy loads of guilt, shame, and regret. You do not need this baggage. It does not serve you. Learn from your mistakes and move on. You have too many important things to do!

This is where energy healing practices such as Reiki and Shamanic journeying can be useful to jumpstart your healing, so you may begin anew every day. You must forgive yourself for your past, so you may finally live in the present moment and enjoy your life today. If you ever feel stuck in a "groundhog day", there may be a few things you need to release from your brain!

Once you take the Oath of Forgiveness, you *choose* to love yourself, rising to the challenges that have kept your greatest desires and wishes from coming true. Leave your trials and tribulations behind and step into the Unknown as the courageous leader you are at your core.

When you align with The Way, others may look to you for guidance. You may become a guidepost—a torch with the power to light The Way for others. You are blessed in ways you cannot fathom yet. In time, you will see. Trust the process. Everything is going according to plan for your highest good. Treat your path as if it were the certain way to enlightenment, for it is.

Setting Intentions

The Way is the path of least resistance for achieving your dream life. To consistently manifest things you want (and to slow down the flow of things you do not want), setting intentions is a critical part of this process. You must express *precisely* what you want through your thoughts and feelings if you want them to come forth into physical form.

Identify the core essence of what you want, because you may not have perfectly formed concepts of how you want those things to appear in the physical world. Source will deliver better things than your brain can fathom, if you can get down to the essence of your desires and then remain open to the infinite possibilities (instead of cutting them off by clinging to ideas in your brain). To begin this focusing practice:

Turn Inward upon Waking

A short meditation in the morning is helpful for starting the day in a centered state. This gives you time to focus on your intentions and goals, and to remind yourself of Universal Law so you can consciously manifest the day more easily.

Turn Inward Before Sleeping

It is possible to do this important intention-setting work in your non-waking reality. What intentions would be useful for sleep? Intend to solve a problem you're experiencing and wake up with the answer. Intend to discover how you feel about a sensitive situation or a critical decision that needs your attention. Conquer fears while you sleep, so you can wake up with them erased! Why not? Believe it is possible—your brain is creating your reality, and *you,* as the Great Creator, have the power to make your reality however you'd like it to be. Don't be a slave to your thoughts. This Work is not commonly practiced, but sleep comprises a third of your time here. Why not learn to use it to your greatest advantage?

How to Recognize and Stay in the Flow

Learn to recognize The Flow and ride the wave to get what you're looking for, without hard work. Throughout your days, follow the path of least resistance. Let your day lead you and do not resist changes to your plans—see what happens. This does not mean become passive. Rather, maintain intentionality, but be fluid with unexpected events. All changes happen for a reason.

- Concentrate on what you want, while accepting the present moment for what it is. Think of this process like using a time machine, and the only way to get to where you want to be is to think *very* clearly about where you're going.
- Move with your impulses and intuition to make the most useful decisions.
- Have courage and Know that your wishes will be met, even if not in the way you expect, or in the timeframe you *think* is best. Remember that everything will unfold in the most beneficial way, for you and all of existence.

If your path is unclear, it is not yet time for it to be clear. Just relax and nothing will stand in the way of your heart's desire manifesting. As you remain poised and centered, you will know what to do at each moment.

Universal Law (Again)

Repetition of key lessons is the most integrative way to reset your brain and expectations of life. Without repetition, it would be next to impossible to incorporate these messages into daily living.

- Do unto others as you would have them do unto you (and vice versa).
- Behave with kindness, dignity, and honor.
- Have respect for yourself and all others.
- Show courage when others are fearful, compassion when others are weak, and nobility when nothing is asked for.
- Avoid rash decisions and substances which may cause rash

behavior.
- Regret nothing, but move forward with precision and certainty, keeping an eye out for any ego activity.
- Cherish this moment. It ought to be your best.
- You are as perfect as you have ever been, now.
- Treat *all* of physical reality as you would your child or work of art.

These laws are not "commandments," but rather they are *guidelines* you may choose to follow if you desire greatness beyond the physical rat race you have witnessed. It is up to you how you choose to conduct yourself in this lifetime, but it is by these moral standards that the greatest leaders and most spiritually renowned citizens of your world choose to live and behave.

Sometimes this path may feel lonely, but only for a short time. That is the mark and the burden which all prominent leaders must face from time to time. Doing things differently from the crowd is challenging sometimes. You may feel as if you don't belong. Persevere. You will be glad you did.

Doubt vs. Clarity

Once you taste Truth, it cannot be denied. There will be nothing to question. If you have doubts, that is a hint something is amiss—something is worth inspecting. Do not jump to conclusions about problems or sensitive matters, in your personal life or on a political or global scale (especially since you are only seeing from your limited perspective).

It is your right to seek answers about complicated problems to help broaden your perspective or to clear from your mind negative opinions or judgments. This is why it is important to maintain openness to all things and all possibilities, no matter what your current impression is (especially in places where great power is held or vast sums of money accumulate).

Do not be fooled if you have doubts in your heart about complicated or strange situations that pop up in your life, or in regard to political "sides" constructed by the media. Learn *not* to ignore your doubts. Seek Truth within and you will no longer find yourself participating in the battlefields of politics and religion.

If any unclear situation requires your extensive compassion (e.g. if someone has lied to you, a group of people has been labeled an "enemy," or a societal problem has caused disruption in your life), it becomes easier to deploy heart-centered energy toward another *if you have remained open and heart-centered the whole time*. Do your best not to close yourself off using popular labels or belief systems (the media develops many of these). It is important to remember that each person you encounter is, at their core, a Divine Creator, but perhaps they haven't realized it yet. What a revelation it will be when they finally see!

Relaxation and Patience

You do not need to hurry through every day. In fact, it is best to relax. Go with the flow. Develop a greater capacity to hold tranquility so you are more confident when faced with uncertainty.

Patience is a virtue not commonly mastered, which is why the world appears the way it does. When you maintain a broader perspective (particularly during stressful situations), things operate more smoothly. When you view life from confined levels of awareness, things do not always appear smooth (in fact, they may appear pretty rough!).

In many situations, it takes more time than expected to achieve the desired results, causing you to lose track of the bigger picture and panic or give up. When events take an unexpected turn for the "worse," and you aren't consciously sitting in your center, you may self-sabotage with beliefs that these observed imperfections will never change or get better (creating stress and further impatience).

Practice "zooming out" on your problems when things do not appear to be flowing the way you *think* they should. Once you are aligned and willing to trust The Way, you will more likely remember your patience through uncertain life changes, allow them to pan out without your inward personal bias or added resistance, and you will more frequently enjoy the deep peace and relaxation for which many people search.

Remember to breathe deeply. Enjoy your time. It is not possible to rush the unfolding, and it will get to you no matter what state it finds you in. You might as well be well-rested, relaxed, and happy, right? Picture a cartoon character running frantically in place, the carpet piling up behind him like an accordion, versus the same character walking leisurely down the carpet. The unfolding moves at its own pace, so when you work yourself into a frenzy trying to get things to happen, that only creates gray hair and annoyance. All you need to do is ride the wave, as cool and calm as you'd like, and you'll find yourself making more progress toward your goals than most.

> *Fear not the Unknown, for that is where great mystery and excitement derive. What would life be without it?*

Inner Guidance

The inner world has ways of communicating with you when you least expect it. When you are searching for clarity, certain animals may cross your path, perhaps several times in a short period. You can encounter these creatures in your physical reality, in a dream, in a text or image, or in audio form. Various cultures have assigned meaning to these experiences relative to the inner world and everyday life. Use these animals or symbols or synchronicities as a reminder to become aware of your thoughts and feelings, especially when you find yourself caught in your external minutiae.

Enlightenment

Enlightenment is an infinite path of increasing inner clarity. Few have achieved great strides on this Path. It is attainable, but requires great dedication, courage, and daily practice. You must be present, always willing to listen to your inner guidance (rather than your ego). Once you achieve this (at least sometimes), all your wishes will manifest. That is Law. Enjoy the path Home.

Contemplations

- Which two of your addictive tendencies or bad habits do you dislike the most?
- What can you do to shift your focus from one of these? When will you start? Lay out small (daily) goals for yourself and achieve them one at a time. No need to climb a mountain without forging a simple path first.

- What is the number one biggest mistake in your past that you have not forgiven yourself for?
- Why are you holding on to it? Has the experience helped you avoid making additional mistakes?
- What are two new ways you can respect yourself? What can you do, just for you, that will help you feel more in control and aligned with your standards?
- What animal have you noticed crossing your path? Look up its spiritual meaning and see if it coincides with a problem you've been experiencing, or an aspect of your character you've been developing.
- How often do you choose to focus only on things you dislike? What would it take for you to focus on the aspects of your life and yourself you are proud of?

3

Inner Freedom

Inner freedom is a desirable feeling tone, a very clear frequency, not yet fully realized or enjoyed by most of the human population. It takes courage to traverse the coarse inner path to get to the place where one genuinely and *effortlessly* does not care what other people think (not just pretending, like most of us). When you have found this inner space, it becomes exciting to step forth into the Unknown with passion and great desire to create.

Through the training of the brain, there becomes no need to worry about the uncertainty of success. You discover that fears are like a cloud of dust you can simply bypass. You will have no reason to develop negative feelings about the uncanny, surprising results (perhaps labeled as failure) from a ridiculous experiment turned into a mess. It is always good information after all!

So, how can you develop this clear state of awareness? Daily reminders are helpful, such as the exercise listed below. It is also imperative that you fully ground yourself into your body any way you find enjoyable: baths, dry brushing, massages, body work like tai chi, yoga, dancing, exercising, etc.

Freedom Breath Exercise

To continue your journey back to your full sense of freedom (which is your birthright), do this exercise at least two or three times in a row, especially when you're faced with an undesirable situation that is not your idea of what you'd like your life to look like:

- Close your eyes
- Breathe in deeply
- Exhale fully
- Repeat this to yourself: *"I am where I need to be. Everything has a purpose."*

While you may not want to believe this statement now, over time, you will see why and how this is true. This exercise, if done regularly, will affect your body on all levels, enhancing relaxation and recalibrating your energy system back into harmony with the way things *are*. It will help you to refocus your perception of any situation and unwind any undesirable beliefs you've been holding on to for too long.

> *Freedom is the carefree expression of one's True Self, with no shame, no guilt, and no resistance to what may happen as a result of showing one's soul to the world.*

Financial Freedom

Freedom is the feeling you get when the pursuit of money is no longer a hindrance to your fullest, most unique expression. It is *free* to imagine that you have already achieved your most extravagant financial goals, and it is imperative that you generate a feeling of "monetary abundance" *within* yourself as often as possible to shift your belief systems closer to what you really want. A fun way to do this is to play the Billionaire's Club.

Billionaire's Club

- Get a pen and notebook and find a comfortable place to sit alone or with a group.
- Take a few moments and imagine that you have $1 billion (or more) right this very second. Take enough time so you feel a shift in your mind and heart space (this is the "freedom feeling" we're talking about). You'll know it when you feel it. You might get chills or butterflies. Your heart rate might increase, in a good way.
- Start writing a list of *all* the things you will buy and activities you will do, knowing you have this financial security. Share with the group if you want to. Have fun with it! **IMPORTANT: Do not censor yourself**! Write every single, silly little thing down, even if it comes across as "shallow" or unimportant. *None* of your desires are unimportant—that Ferrari, a closet full of Jimmy Choos, a trip to a nice palm tree with all of your favorite people—each one of these desires needs to be given room for you to feel full, content, and excited about life.

Keep in mind the Law that you may not harm another person or hinder another person's full expression without detrimental consequence. Bear in mind too, we are not suggesting you need these physical things to be happy or content. What we're doing here is getting to the bottom of what your soul desires to express. So, by writing everything down, you make space within yourself to see your soul's desires more clearly.

- As you continue writing your list, you will inevitably unearth your deeper desires—some that perhaps you have not been paying attention to. You will understand yourself better and may come up with new ideas for how you could achieve some of these things on your list without one billion dollars.
- Keep this list until your next game session. Edit it whenever you feel bored or inspired to work on it.

Whichever item stands out the most as your greatest desire right now, start brainstorming ways you could make it happen (or at least start making daily progress on it) with the resources you have today. If you have too much resistance about it happening with your current financial situation, you can at least remember that since you've now asked for it, with more precision, the universe will reveal the path to it soon! Continue focusing on the excitement of this goal *daily* and remember to be open to the infinite possibilities of *how* it may show up in physical form. It may be nothing like what you imagine.

* * *

To have everlasting life, you must learn to access the freedom (or rather, a more accurate comprehension of reality) deep within your soul. To achieve and maintain the *full* feeling of freedom for long periods of time requires the Daily Work. Attempting to capture this freedom solely within the external world, such as flying around in an airplane or jumping out into the sky, will only carry you so far. The brief spurts of freedom you can achieve while taking part in high-adrenaline sports, for example, are only surface deep. Doing the work within is the only way to experience a pure and unwavering sense of freedom.

Once you connect with Source energy, you will Know yourself better and develop an ever-greater sense of self-worth, self-confidence, and self-respect. You will build a foundation upon which to appreciate the freedom you already have access to whenever you desire to enjoy it. If you have not yet tasted the exquisite depths of this joyous experience, you have so much to look forward to!

Your Birthright

Everyone has access to freedom from birth. It is your birthright to be free and to express yourself fully. The illusion of freedom taken from one Being by another is a crime against humanity, and perpetrators will be dealt with, either by the higher courts, or better yet, by their own moral compass, no matter how much a criminal of this sort has suppressed or ignored their crimes against another.

Do not compromise this vital, life-giving birthright. Do not trade it for anything. *Nothing* is worth the sacrifice of your unique expression—that type of sacrifice will kill you from the inside out. It is your number one priority on this planet to express your unique factor, so you *must* commit to yourself and to your freedom. Where you find this sense of freedom is where you will also have clear access to Truth. This is where true power derives, and no one may take it from you. They may try to distract you, but that's all they can do.

This cherished trait must be protected and allowed to flourish in young children, so they may grow into the rich, unique Beings they will sprout into naturally, as Source intended all along. Do not starve their light or cover it up—it is fragile in childhood. Protect it. That is your duty as a good parent. Protect the light within your children until it grows into its own strong flame of Truth and Understanding.

Importance of Relaxation

To harness inner freedom, you must relax. Relaxing becomes a challenge when you are preparing, consciously or subconsciously, for a perceived disaster at home or at work, or for example, when a new relationship comes into the picture. If the mind is not trained to remain in the present moment, it will busy itself to find something to stress about. If there is not something stressful occurring around you, your brain may find stressful situations in its memory bank or will imagine what could happen in the future. This is a survival mechanism that does not function as intended in the modern-day civilized world. The human body is not designed to withstand "stress preparedness" twenty-four-seven.

You are always on the move, ready for action, but when you successfully relax, you may discover there is no need for action. The type of action we speak of here is the type which comes from a place of fear and insecurity – *forced* action. Forced action cuts you off from what you desire most: freedom and love. Attaining these does not require fearful, resistant, or rushed action, but rather a pause in the egocentric rhythm of life, to allow All That Is to flow through you, so you may realize Oneness once again. This is why beginning and ending each day with meditation is so critically important.

We are not saying "do not act." Allowing the flow to "flow through" means doing the actions which seem natural or obvious in the moment. Meditation provides you with the clarity to step forward each day in the best direction, which may not have been so clear had you not gifted yourself a few quiet minutes in the beginning of the day to realign to your soul mission and excitement for life, releasing excessive resistance.

Questions to Consider

I'm Not Good Enough

Do you often feel inadequate? This pattern, including any accompanying destructive thoughts, usually stems from childhood. Begin by remembering *you are enough.* There is no need to do certain things in order to be more interesting or what have you. Meditate on this feeling to see what memories surface. Once you find the childhood root, look your unloved child-self in the eye and tell them you love them and they have always been enough. Forgive yourself. A photo from around age five is helpful for this exercise.

What Did She Say?

Do you worry about what other people think or say about you? This is likely another child part of you that has not healed from an embarrassing or traumatic situation. This is another wounded place inside you asking for your forgiveness. It may be comforting to remember that you need not fret over false perceptions of Truth, whatever that may mean to you: gossip, lies… The Truth will always win out in the end. Thus, relaxing is a more constructive use of time than worrying about what *he said she said*. It is much more enjoyable to be a human *being* and cease being a human *doing*, or a human worrying!

Grudge Blankies

Do you carry around self-destructive baggage from your past? Inner certainty and clarity are achieved in the process of letting go. All the stressors and baggage most people drag around for no reason other than self-misery and self-sabotage do not help you. They weigh you down and slow your progress toward enlightenment and achieving your greatest goals. They also enhance the aging process. You must let *all* of that go. Relax into each moment. Enjoy life. That is part of the purpose of being here, isn't it? Are you enjoying the ride? Or are you playing the victim card most of the time? Explore your childhood some more and see where you can finally let old grudges go.

Boredom

Boredom is a state of stuck energy. It is filled with old, stagnant things that need to be removed so you may feel your innate freedom and curiosity. If you do not feel free, you are blocking that channel. It is your job—your obligation to yourself—to find the block and remove it so you can get back to your naturally precise frequency which facilitates further enlightenment. No one can do this for you. Keep in mind, it is not enough to clear this channel once. You must be thorough and have enough self-respect to clear the channel as much as is necessary. Morning meditation will become your most useful maintenance protocol for this too.

Boredom Clearing Exercise

Here is one method to remove a mid-day block (or at least discover what is causing it):

- Sit on the couch, eyes closed. Have a pen and paper close by.
- Wait until the block clears. This could take several minutes. Let your mind wander, but do your best not to latch on to any one thought strongly or for too long. If you start making a mental list of the things you forgot to do or need to do tomorrow, write them down to clear them. Then start again.
- This may develop into a brainstorming session. What are you doing with your life? Where are you going? And no, we don't mean get sucked into a whirlwind of self-sabotage and misery with past regrets or fingers pointed. What

excites you right *now*? Figure it out! What else is there to do? If you feel excited about an idea, let it flow until you're ready to jump off the couch and do it.
- Another option is to do a quick five-minute workout. Do a couple push ups or sit ups. Look up a video to guide you through an exercise that will get your heart moving. Stagnancy of the mind is enhanced by stagnancy of the heart and body. We recommend including some form of exercise in your daily routine to avoid this (it doesn't need to be excessive).

* * *

Be Full of Yourself

Being "full of yourself" is used as an insult, perhaps because it's actually a desirable state to be in and most people don't know how to genuinely do it. Most of us are like Swiss cheese, full of holes and energy leaks, and so we look to others to fill us. If someone has looked within, and they can be genuinely "full" rather than empty, bravo, what an achievement! That feeling serves as a reminder that you are one complete Soul Being, whole and perfect as you are. You will not feel empty. You will feel content. There is no room for emptiness if you are at home within yourself. That is where freedom and power exist.

The Art of Expression

Expression is an art-form that cannot be denied its full potential without consequence. Denying or restricting your or someone else's unique expression creates resistance within space-time reality, which hinders growth and overall development (not only for you, the Creator denying your own divine freedom, but for all of existence). Existence does not live up to its greatest potential without you being your best you.

To enjoy freedom of expression (if you have deviated far off your path and do not know how you want to express at this point) you must delve into the depths of your soul. These words may only take you so far on this quest. Do not be discouraged if answers do not appear immediately in your meditation practice. You must re-sensitize to your inner Knowing so that ideas for your exquisite expression flow easily. This path comes with rich rewards and will keep you coming back for more, Knowing that you will become more aligned the further you go…. so be patient! The Way will always become clear when you are ready.

Nature provides many perfect, unique expressions of Source, none of which have the desire or capacity to alter their expression to benefit another. For example, the great willow tree exudes quite a prominent feeling tone. As an observer of such an element of nature, you may be overcome by the desire to relax, for this tree is the most graceful of them all, always standing tall, unable to hide, unable to cover up its scars. It remains centered in itself – its frequency does not change, for its unique vibrational signature is optimal for its greatest expression. You would never ask the willow tree to change, would you? Bear this in mind when you feel the need to change for others, or if you desire others to change for you. To try to change who you are or to cover your True Self is unproductive if you want to evolve. This resistance to yourself reduces peace and harmony within the cosmos, creates unnecessary pain and suffering, and thus is a disservice to you and to all of existence (this is the root cause of much illness).

Only you can express your unique factor, and by denying the expression of such, the universe and Source are, by definition, not expressing their perfection completely. You will not feel free if you Know you are not being your True Self. All Beings on this planet are One overall expression, and each must applaud all other expressions in whatever shape or form they appear. How can one judge another based on a limited perspective? True freedom of expression ought to be cherished and honored, for it is by this path that you may do as you please (so long as you do not hinder or harm another creative Being, of course).

> *Forge your own path and you will flourish.*

Contemplations

- What is one current situation you feel tense about that you can, right now, allow yourself to relax about, remembering that all things happen as they need to?
- Are you enjoying your time? If you are going with the flow, you have no reason not to enjoy every waking moment.
- Try imagining, for three full minutes, that you have $1 billion right now. How does it make you feel?
- Can you carry this feeling with you through one day this

week and see how it affects the day overall?
- Identify one time you felt like a victim or when you "pointed fingers." Can you think of another way to view this situation, whereby you are not giving your inner power away to someone else? Pointing fingers is just that: giving your power away to another, so you can avoid blame or responsibility for your feelings, or for how your life is going, or to ignore the fact that you *allowed* someone to cross your boundaries. This only delays your enjoyment of life!

4

Fear

Fear is quite useful in live-or-die situations, but as this world moves into higher planes of awareness, our awareness of fear must evolve along with us, not as something to discard or run away from. In the civilized world, the purpose of fear is not to turn you away from challenges that would, in fact, assist in your evolution of self-awareness. Fear is meant to be a signaling device, to shed light on areas in life where a misperception exists that would be best to inspect, or areas that would actually be enjoyable to further express into. Once you begin exploring this great asset, you will see opportunities enjoyed only by those brave enough to face their fears.

Fear is a powerful tool that can be used to guide you toward your inner light, your purest, cleanest Source frequency. If left unchecked, it has the potential to be detrimental to your health and happiness. Do not worry so much about short-term fears. The problems (and opportunities) lie with the gripping, illogical, loathing, long-standing fears that have accumulated power over your soul and well-being. You would do well to identify and take care of these.

You may feel some level of fear and discomfort while experiencing significant changes in life. Use deep breathing and the Daily Work to ensure a smooth transition. You will be fine. Do not live out your days in fear—instead, face the world with courage, strength, and honesty. The potential within you is strong and true. You can change the world for the better.

> *Once you face your fears, they begin to disappear.*

Fear Elimination Exercise

Fear can be complicated, but facing it is the best way to understand where you need to work on yourself to accelerate your growth, and to make your life the way you want it to be. This is one of your most important responsibilities. To get a better handle on your fears, use the following exercise:

- Sit alone in a quiet place, with a notebook and pen.
- Close your eyes and brainstorm about what scares you the most.
- Make a list of everything that pops into your mind.
- Are any of these fears related in some way? Perhaps by a similar thought pattern or belief about yourself?
- Spend time contemplating these to gain clarity on the root of the fear(s) and determine why they are there. Are they simply outdated bad habits, or are they left from an unprocessed traumatic event? Is there a neglected or child part of you that needs your love or forgiveness?

- Once you identify a fear or a fearful thought pattern weaved through your list, the best thing you can do is approach it in an incremental, un-shocking manner, one step at a time.

The fearful moments you encounter in your life can be seen as growth opportunities. As you expand your awareness of your fears and of yourself, you will be able to face these things in your daily life with more confidence.

To turn away from fear is to turn away from yourself. By giving power to your fears, you are hindering your expansion and giving your power away to something outside of you. It may not be clear yet how to approach a fear comfortably, but as long as you are determined to eliminate it, the universe will reveal the path soon enough. You must only ride the wave! Life is meant to be enjoyed and honored for the challenges it offers for your expansion. What's not to love in this world of things that get messed up?

Worldwide Fear

Fear can get out of hand and become a problem for entire communities, countries, and even the whole human race. Fear of change, and maybe a bit of laziness, leads to the clinging to out-of-date technologies for years and decades to the detriment of society. While new discoveries may cause large-scale shifts in infrastructure, for civilization to move forward, transformation must occur. How about those free energy devices?

Fear has the power to shut down an entire planet, bringing royalty to their knees, begging and pleading for someone to stop this dis-ease. Little do they know that the perfect world they've wanted is within their grasp… and has been all along. But when someone, or a group of someones, creates an idea of a perfect world, and pushes for it to come forth, regardless of the clear signs from above that it is not beneficial for anyone involved, it is this sneaky element of fear that manifests as a desperate need to control one's surroundings, perhaps derived from the fear to survive, and ultimately the fear of death. This alone has been the linchpin of all the undoing of the Garden.

Perhaps some people think that going back to the way things once were would put us back into this perfect state of peace and harmony, but in Reality, existence as we know it is transforming through time, and we will never, ever go backwards and achieve any sort of benefit from that. Moving forward through our fears of the Unknown is always the best move in this never-ending game of chess.

Fear creates *texture* in the void of time and space, to show contrast in a world that desires everything to remain unchanged. Fear provides *opportunity* to develop courage and strength, and without these jolting calls to action, there would be no inner traction toward growth or change.

Fear can pull you in and convince you of a reality that doesn't exist, and never did. It is up to you to *see for yourself* and understand Truth for what it is—and is not. How do you handle your fears? Do you seem to conquer them and then drawback here and there? As you see these drawbacks becoming less frequent and extreme, be assured you are making progress.

Fears are part of your journey within, and to clear your inner clutter, you must walk through them, or at least edge the lawn to start. Then you may help others if it becomes necessary.

Protect Your Children

Parents sometimes use fear to motivate their children, which must be done with great care, for when used excessively, it can smother the flame of uniqueness within them. Fear is meant to be a *guide*, not a rod of punishment.

Children are meant to express themselves freely. They are born with their own mission and goals for expansion, and as they develop and explore their souls, their fears will be revealed, identifying the parts of them that are ripe for development or blossoming. It is the parents' job to create the right growing environment from which they can explore these areas in a safe, productive manner. Conquering fears does not need to feel equivalent to jumping off a cliff.

When your child comes face-to-face with a fear, such as stage fright, develop with them some sort of game like a mountain climbing map, with goals and treasures along the way. Decide with them what would be the easiest way to begin their quest up this mountain of fear, like making a speech in front of two friends, and then three.

Far too many grown adults have such a massive fear of rejection, which becomes a great hindrance to life and self-expression. Working with a child who doesn't yet have an established fear-based root system will give them a great boost in life that is hard to imagine!

Benefits of Fear

Fear is the mechanism by which you may develop courage. It is not evil or an enemy; it serves a most noble purpose for all Beings in this reality. Fear may cause you to cling to a stagnant, safe reality. Yet, when your safe little world unexpectedly comes crashing down, you may notice all your fears go along with it. What becomes of you after disaster, death, or a life-changing experience is where the magic exists and is where you can courageously start over, refine your ability to lead your Universe—your Kingdom—which is your primary duty and obligation. Fear will always be there to nudge you and keep you on your toes, and once you maintain awareness of its purpose, you will always know the direction that is most beneficial for you to go, just like the yellow brick road.

Fear itself is an illusion based on false perceptions or misperceptions of Truth, so do not fret about the past or what might be in the future. Fear can slow you down and cause you to hesitate, so be brave! Know the Universe is bringing you everything you ask for, whether or not you realize it. Honor yourself, be courteous to all others, and you will have nothing to fear.

> *Fear not the Unknown, for that is where you will find your greatest treasures. Take hold of adventure, seek your answers deep within, and you will be well satisfied.*

Vulnerability

To achieve greatness requires strength and courage. You may practice and build courage by facing your fears and learning to keep your system open and vulnerable when it is safe to do so. When you feel that curtain of fear come before you in a situation, you have a choice in that moment to either close your system, resist the experience, and continue following your self-limiting belief systems, or, you can keep your system open and allow your energy to flow through the fear cloud. You will experience great rewards when you choose the new path.

Vulnerability is a choice you make within yourself. Choosing to be emotionally *open* in a sensitive situation is rarely a bad choice (provided, of course, you are in an environment that is not abusive). By being vulnerable emotionally, ie. opening your heart, you allow your soul to express itself fully. If you choose to live within the bounds of your fears, like a rat in the rat race, you will progressively cut yourself off from your source of joy and the awareness of who you are and your greater purpose. This has a tendency to manifest into disease, not to mention depression and lack of fulfillment. Consider poor physical and mental health side effects of you pampering your fears and not following the desires of your True Self.

Choosing vulnerability creates great strength of character. You cannot Know the boundless treasures that are waiting for you unless you face your challenges head on. Filet your soul to the world, so to speak, and you will comprehend the power of this choice.

The road less followed (The Way) is rarely chosen because it requires such a high degree of vulnerability, dedication, and courage—and a conscious decision to do things in your unique way, without fear of rejection. This leaves you open to attack. Others may question your lifestyle. They may feel jealousy, anger, contempt. Keep in mind, however, that strong emotional reactions from others may signal that you are steering in the right direction. After all, if you were not following Inner Truth, no one would think twice about your decisions. People perk up when, deep down, they Know you are doing the work they have been avoiding. Jealousy and hatred directed at you from another person are two excellent indicators of this.

> *Haters gonna hate.*

Be a guidance system for those around you who seek Truth. Bear witness only to the Truth of existence, which at its core is love, harmony, and balance. Persevere. Haters may appear for a brief time. Consider them bits of dust left in your energy field. They will clear out if you sustain the cleaner frequency you establish by following The Way.

Develop Depth of Character

To develop real depth of character requires time, dedication, finesse, and courage… so be prepared to face your fears and weaknesses. What's there to lose? You must put in the work required, rather than being lazy or shying away from challenges. It is in the challenges of life that character is built best.

Some challenges are thrust upon us unexpectedly, but you may also create enjoyable challenges that engage and strengthen the parts of yourself you know need work. It is up to you to go out, or in, and face yourself.

Do not be scared away, thinking you must face your greatest fears unprepared. It is most enjoyable to start small, then chip away at your monstrous fears. You might discover a way to approach fear so that it doesn't affect you, like breaking each one down into manageable steps until they are no longer a threat.

True depth of character is developed in moments of weakness when you discover parts of yourself that you never knew existed. That is the road to greatness, whether or not you can see it yet. Trust The Way, for it holds wonderful mysteries and excitement for your pure enjoyment. Let your inner guidance lead the way as you bear witness to the glory that unfolds before you. Choose to treat others with courtesy and respect, behave with honor and dignity, and you will travel through this life well.

Release Excessive Resistance

Remember to let the unfolding occur as it will, and do not control things out of fear, for that creates resistance against the flow. Do your best not to be alarmed by change, but instead embrace it with delight. Releasing tension and conscious relaxation will help you face your fears and improve your health (while also minimizing gray hairs and wrinkles…).

Do your best not to worry about the past and do not harm yourself by recreating the past in your present moment. You wouldn't dump your kitchen garbage all over your living room rug every time it was full, would you? That is equivalent to dragging past regrets, pain, money problems, and failures into your present thoughts. If you want to repeat those experiences, continue thinking about how bad they were and how much you suffered like victims do! They will repeat in one form or another.

Cherish every moment, for each is a blessing, even if well-disguised in fear or failure. Know that you are a Divine Creator, here to create greatness in what may appear to be a land of despair. You are doing well. Nothing will stand in your way to true happiness, for you have within you the secret to achieving all the fulfillment you could ever want (and more). People may look to you for guidance, and you will be well equipped to help them.

Contemplations

- If you often feel powerless, how many external things have you given your power away to (i.e. what circumstances or people do you blame your misery on, or what things do you point to when you think about your life not being the way you want)? Make a list. How can you take responsibility for these things? That is one way you can change your reality.
- What is the first fear you're going to explore? Why do you think this is a fear for you in the first place? It's important to get to the root of this *why*, because if you can clear up the originating factor, it will dissipate much more easily.
- Where in your past have you avoided being vulnerable?
- Have you ever wanted to tell someone you loved them, but held back out of fear of rejection? It's helpful to remember that we can love another, and enjoy those feelings for ourselves, without *needing* them to reciprocate. The *need* for them to reciprocate is a signal that you are not filling yourself with love, and this has the tendency to deter the other from participating in such a potentially codependent or parasitic experience. The fear of them not reciprocating causes us to stop our own flow of energy, which has a negative impact on our health and happiness. A wise person once said, "If you love it, let it go". You may love

and enjoy love without clinging to an outcome. This is a skill that must be developed with the heart.

- Have you ever avoided telling someone how you felt about something they did that hurt you? In these types of situations, being vulnerable and honest allows you to avoid a buildup of resentment. Let your true feelings flow, and you will feel much better, regardless of the outcome. Do your best, of course, to deliver your expression as peacefully and compassionately as you can muster, so as not to cause a bigger mess, but instead cleans up what is left from the past. This is good boundary healing work.

5

True Love

The reason we signify this as "true love" rather than just simply "love" is because, quite often, what we *think* is love is really a concept coming from the brain, rather than being derived fully from the heart.

You can think of the brain as a highly advanced, artificial intelligence creation facility, which is quite magnificent since it is connected to the heart by way of the whole physical body. Nothing can compare to this exquisite design—it is unmatched and perhaps shall remain so until the end of time.

Nonetheless, the most commonly known problem with this highly advanced system is that its operators —the human race— have not learned to intelligently operate these vehicles. Most end up fully existing inside of the brain cavity and have not yet explored the other areas of the body, which would indeed give them the tools they've been missing, to live the life of their dreams, of course.

So how indeed do we occupy the rest of these sacred vehicles of light? It requires daily focused attention on this matter— dedicated time getting to know yourself better, to come to know each part intimately. Each part has a consciousness and will teach you what it needs to operate in harmony with the rest of the system.

The real driver's seat —the real command center— where you may access your Throne, is known as the Heart Center. The point to be focused upon exists at the base of the heart, because this Heart Center is not merely the center of your organ heart, but rather it comprises the heart, heart chakra, the heart's roots, and part of the solar plexus region.

Seated firmly in your Throne, you will have full access to love and joy. You will not be identifying with the ego here, but instead you'll be in a place to witness it, appreciate the work you've done on it, and see what yet needs further sculpting. For, the ego is a divine work of art—your greatest masterpiece in the making. It needs your true love.

The next benefit of finding this perfectly centered and grounded place is the love you will feel for yourself and for all of your self-labeled mistakes. You will have full access to compassion for everyone in your life, including family members. You will see your Path of Purpose, your path to self forgiveness, your path to greater self awareness, your path to deeper fulfillment, exquisite romantic partnership, and at that instant, you will be living in the present moment.

So as you can see, there are innumerable reasons why operating from this Heart Center is so vital to humanity at large. This is the next step in human evolution—to get out of the brain and to come back Home to the Heart.

* * *

True love is desired by all on this planet, so it serves as an excellent catalyst for inner growth and total transformation. Many a man and woman can attest to being transformed after being in a relationship, with all of its tests and catastrophes, and perhaps miseries. Whether the relationship fails or becomes stronger doesn't reveal how much inner work has been accomplished along the way.

True love is one of the best, if not *the* best, catalyst for action in an opposite or unexpected direction—so much so that someone may be thrust into facing a fear that only a year ago felt like a momentous, horrific danger.

There is more to true love than just desire. It is a practice, a commitment, first to yourself, and then perhaps to another. It is meant to be cherished. It is meant to be honored. It is meant to be remembered without a reminder.

Once you have felt true love, you will never be the same. It will leave you feeling content with life as it *is*, for it helps you regain perspective on which aspects of life are *really* important, and which should be eliminated or changed.

Self-Love

If you've ever felt empty, want to know what you're missing? It is you, yourself. Want to know what will make you happy and fulfilled? You, yourself. Want to know where true love originates and finds its most genuine expression? It is within you, yourself. It is up to you to deepen that understanding to experience the greatest pleasure in all of life.

To attain the ability to love with great depth requires more inner work than most people realize or perhaps are willing to do. As you become unafraid to explore the depths of your soul, you will have capacity to love yourself more, and thus, your ability to give love and receive love from others, such as your beloved partner, will exceed even your wildest imaginings for what a soul-bonded partnership could create and be, as a power couple and team.

How to Increase Self-Love

"Love yourself" is such a worn-out thing to say, yet most people have not grasped this concept beyond surface level. Self-love is needed more now than ever before, yet few people take it seriously. How on earth can you commit to another human being if you're not willing to put forth the effort to love yourself first? To develop true, deep self-love is a lifelong commitment and requires the Daily Work. To begin this most important self-discovery process:

- Sit quietly with yourself daily, in the morning and at night. Just a few minutes is all it takes. This was mentioned earlier—it's an important habit! Use shamanic drumming if you need help to focus. Write down your daily tasks for your most exciting goals, and contemplate your life every night by a fire or with eyes closed.
- Try new things. You cannot get excited, with or without a relationship, if you do not know what excites you. Explore the world via traveling, classes, sports, going to shows, concerts, meet up groups, challenge yourself, discover your strengths and weaknesses, learn to accept yourself as you are. The more you try new things, the more you remind your brain that you don't know "everything," change is normal, the world is bigger than you can imagine, and everything is okay. The more you do this, the better and

deeper you will be able to love both yourself and others. So, by making more time for yourself, everyone benefits. There isn't a better win-win scenario.
- Commit to doing the best you can every moment, no matter how insignificant your actions seem. Every single thing that happens in your life is beneficial to you in some capacity, whether that be actions which move you swiftly in your desired direction, or mistakes which give you a clearer outline of your path via "data collection". To truly commit to yourself requires intention, dedication, courage, and great self-respect. Be the best you can be for nobody but yourself, because you are *that* important, whether you recognize it or not.

To commit to another person is impossible if one has not committed to oneself, first and foremost. It is of vital importance to humanity (and to all of existence) that we each dedicate time to do this inner work. Only then may we properly take care of ourselves and evolve in an enjoyable manner.

> *Go with what life hands you, one step at a time, with your greatest desires at the back of your mind, and day by day you will begin to see the perfection of your masterpiece come to be.*

Start treating yourself as if you have your dream relationship. Keep your home feeling good, whether or not there is someone there with you—light candles, clean, declutter, make nice meals, play music, dress well, keep things fresh. Take pride in what you do for yourself. Take yourself out.

Keep in mind also that the body is your soul's perfect masterpiece. It deserves to be cherished and treated as the work of art it is. It's your greatest creation on this planet after all—your soul's densest expression. It is a holy temple, not a trash bag!

Loving ourselves takes at least as much effort as loving someone else. After we have developed greater self-commitment, we can more easily attract someone of equal caliber, to bond in profound ways most cannot even comprehend.

Commitment

What does it take to Know, without question, that you have found a partnership that will win out in the end? Is it luck? Is it fate? Or is it by design? Perhaps you Know deep in your heart that this is "the one" to carry you through eternity, that your love will outlast the entire physical world, as pure as immortality. *How do you know?*

To be frank, if you are asking that question, you are not in the right state of mind to answer that question. If you desire an answer that will outlast your thoughts, it must not come from the brain, but rather, it must come from the heart. Love is not based on thought alone, and while commitment is a conscious choice for you to make, it is not a choice to be made using your brain.

Use your heart for matters of love—and you will not be disappointed in your results. Any choices and love-based decisions that come solely from the brain spell *catastrophe*… and you will not enjoy the resulting chaos or potential misery! Just remember, your heart Knows what will make you happy. Your brain is there to make those things a reality—it is not there to decide what must be done. Relying on the brain is where mistakes and resistance stem from.

To master this ability to gain insight from the heart requires some work at the front-end, for it is like training a new muscle to do things you've perhaps never done.

- Focus your attention on the base of your heart.
- Ask your question about love or a relationship problem.
- Sit patiently and wait for the answer to come. Use a shamanic drumming track if you need help focusing.
- If clarity does not come in a timely manner, it is perhaps not yet time for you to have your answer. But, the answer may appear in your daily life if you're paying close enough attention.

It is important to be clear here when we say the heart will help you make these important decisions. When the heart makes decisions, these are *not* decisions made on a whim based on emotional reactions. These are **not** decisions caused by a flush of hormones, lust, or base physical desires. Christ consciousness, your connection to Source, [or insert your preferred identifier] resides within the heart field, and as you develop your ability to reveal your fire, become truly heart-centered, recognize and operate in this clean, grounded place, you will be naturally confident in your actions and decisions about commitment. You will make decisions easily, but they will be made from a deep place of true Inner Knowing—pure, untainted wisdom.

No Strings

Could a bond exist between two people whereby, instead of clinging to each other, they would stand as two whole Beings who choose to stand together simply in awe of the other's greatness? Is this how true love thrives: when two souls recognize their autonomous nature, and coexist purely in admiration and bliss at the sight of their partner's equal commitment to achieving greatness in a world of uncertain darkness?

To have a successful partnership and marriage, one must commit, take charge, have the utmost respect at all times, and know when to disengage… True love can be effortless in this state. It requires no games, yet relationships take time and patience, and should always provide space to grow and become better the next day. To birth a family under these circumstances provides a stable foundation upon which a child may learn that *anything* desired may be achieved, so long as the work is done within, first and foremost.

Teaching a child to explore the inner depths of their soul from a young age allows them to maintain the self-recognition they are naturally born with. Most children are deprived of this opportunity, and are treated as lowly members of society, which often results in them covering up and protecting their inner light. This is when they leave the Garden. This is when the aging process begins.

Our bodies are like plants and are fed by the Light of Intelligence[2]—Source. Starve the body of your light, and it will

---

[2] Harold Waldwin Percival, *Thinking and Destiny* (New York: The Word Foundation, Inc., 2006).

die. It will wither up with wrinkles as proof of the resistance and self-created protections and blockages to Inner Truth, and the soul will pass on. If the person never learns how to be self-aware enough to find, harness, and once again reveal their inner light (as they did naturally in childhood), they will not be self-sustaining and will learn to take energy from those around them. As a parent, you can stop this cycle by showing your child how to find their passion and purpose, and to remain in the present moment.

The true love a father and mother have for their children is breathtaking. There are no words to describe the fullness or depth of the love in their hearts. It is *the* pure essence of love in its finest form. But, there are many fine forms in which love can express itself....

Lubricating Perspective

True love is blind and mysterious in some forms, light and feathery in others. It is life's greatest mystery and has left many a man questioning his entire existence. It is seductive and sneaky and can take you by surprise. A tricky little bastard, it's a romantic, inquisitive, feisty little thing sometimes! Yet, it remains honorable above all.

True love is electric and vibrant as it courses through your veins. It is not sticky or stagnant, but resistance can bring this into your relationship if you're missing some lubricating *perspective*. Do your best not to dig yourself into a rut, or cling to your loved ones in fear of losing their love, as true love is abundant and is meant to be enjoyed, not held onto as if you'll somehow miss out on one of life's greatest joys.

A lack of inner security and a scarcity mindset can trigger

some irresponsible feelings like jealousy and rage, self-imposed damnation as an emotional slave... Alas, it all comes back to perspective and conscious awareness of healthy and unhealthy patterns in all of your relationships. How you *choose* to view the world and your life defines your reality.

Fear brings struggle to relationships, too. Sometimes it grips us at the worst possible moment, leaving us feeling blinded or hopeless, when we've simply lost focus. Taking a moment to breathe *alone* is important, to regain perspective on the totality of what's going on (versus what you're imagining). You can indeed transcend things like jealousy and fears of losing your partner, but it requires you to look deep within and heal those fearful patterns.

Don't wait, never hesitate to let your true feelings flow, to see where they might lead you—perhaps through another door, or an open window!

Unconditional love is the most pristine love of them all, but when it is unexpectedly interrupted by tragic loss or catastrophe, this can wreck even the toughest man's heart.

Desirable Nature of Love

Because many people do not love themselves, they seek love outside of themselves, like savage barbarians. But that special, deep, passionate connection with another is so intoxicating, and provides a space to be vulnerable which is often inaccessible within the rest of the world, that no one will ever desire to make a change!

True love is worthy of celebration, and if you do not yet have it, do not fear. You will have your celebration in due time. Fear will not help you achieve what you want, including a loving partner. Treating yourself as royalty provides the backbone and foundation for this whole true love concept to work out. Always remember, you cannot love someone else in a sustainable manner if you do not love yourself first.

Romance

True love is not bound by physical expression alone. It manifests with pure, wholehearted precision on the energetic level, for the benefit of both or one alone. It is important that partners establish and maintain clarity between themselves regarding the direction of the relationship. There must also be agreement on the foundational elements —the morals and values each party brings to the table— as well as all the juicy extras that provide your favorite pleasure. Knowing your desires and being able to verbalize or somehow express these to your partner provides the relationship with a clear path to romantic ecstasy. What do you want?

We all want to experience our most enjoyable intimate physical expressions while developing that ideal, unbreakable, unconditional bond. But why does it seem to be such a challenge to achieve that perfect balance? Expectation creates your manifestation. Do your best to understand yourself, so you may more fully express your needs to your partner, and then you may enjoy more aspects of your partner's true self. Only then can you explore and experience a deeper, more satisfying bond.

> *Let time go by and you will see all your greatest desires come to be. How much time is hard to say, but relax*

yourself, and let come what may.

Know What You Want

A fulfilling and satisfying romantic relationship is the ideal, and if you do not quite have it, it may be because you haven't figured out what it is you want! Again, you must love yourself first. Accept all that you are in the darkest corners of your soul. Only then will you understand what it is you're truly looking for and will be able to accept another into your life, to form a partnership you perhaps never thought was possible.

When choosing your life partner —the one you will confide in, the one you will cry with— the greater your inner clarity, the better. This is no small decision—Lord knows the regrets that have been made with this one! But when you find that person who will love you as you are, no matter what happens, no matter your scars… when you can love each other unconditionally, you may take that as a clear signal from above that you have the power, as a partnership, to make it through it all.

> *Love can be sneaky, as we've said before, ready to attack when you're least ready for her. Love can be sexy (perhaps the most favorite part of all) to take you at your mercy. Regrets? No, no, none at all… Love, let's face it… it's intertwined with fate. It can ruin you or make you great. Regardless, it's here to stay! Choose wisely….*

Partnership

When a woman deeply *trusts* a man to be there for her, to accept all that she is physically, mentally, emotionally, and spiritually, this is all it takes to ignite the King within that man, if he will take on this most honorable challenge. To accomplish this, that man must be willing to fully accept and feel his own emotions, to have the capacity to provide such an atmosphere for total and luxurious letting go and vulnerability for his woman.

Pure and elegant by nature, this bond is fierce and hardy beneath the surface. The foundation of this relationship cannot crack when pure intentions and desires are mutual, such as the desire to remain open towards each other regardless of any fears of rejection. To have a healthy relationship, the lines of trust and respect must be clear—then you can form a solid foundation.

A stable, long-lasting partnership is like a load-bearing wall. While it takes additional resources to build it, if done right, it is built to be strong and can sustain some level of unexpected damage (choose your favorite relationship catastrophe—with the proper tools and supports in place, you can weather any storm, and even improve what you've built. Every life situation can be an opportunity for deepening and strengthening your love). Developing a durable bond needn't be more complex than this, so long as both parties are committed to doing whatever it takes to build a powerful family without giving up.

The bond between two lovers ought to be cherished. It is a divine miracle, two deciding to embark on the path of life together, hoping to have a family of their own. There is such fun to be had on this path, yet it is a path with its own set of challenges and difficulties. Do not forget, we are bringing together two distinct Beings on their own separate paths which still need to be upheld. They then may choose the noble task of bringing life onto this planet (which is not a task to be taken lightly). This is a challenge for all involved, we understand, but if you raise your children well, this experience bears the sweetest fruit for the entire world to enjoy. The honor brought to someone in parenthood is difficult to match, for it comes with such an exquisite, genuine reward to see firsthand what one's offspring may bring to the world. It is the most intimate form of creation—a true fountain of joy.

Communication

The lines of communication within a relationship must remain open if each partner wants it to flourish. This is not always easy. It takes great care and commitment from both parties. If there is to be any meaningful and helpful progress, you must both be willing to work on it every day. Remember, you are bringing two distinct Beings together into close quarters, which can cause disturbances. But, those petty differences can remain sublingual if a broad enough perspective is maintained...

Communication on serious fronts creates the backbone of a relationship, like a reinforced concrete foundation. Keep your greatest goals in your sights, both individually and as a duo. Keep your mutual goals fresh and exciting, so you may practice working out challenges together. Whether or not you choose to actively achieve goals together, know this: maintaining directed focus can conquer entire planets. If your partnership can focus on a focused outcome, that will help you get through communication problems and overcome any obstacles.

If you feel that something is missing or that your emotional needs are not being met, share this with your partner. Just be sure you are not pinning excessive responsibilities on them (such as those you should pin on yourself). We seek love from others because we haven't learned to find it within ourselves. While we all have our infinite learning curves to contend with, try not to throw your sense of emptiness onto your partner to fill for you. It may be fun at the beginning for them to do extra things for you to show their love, but it will become tiring and will drain them of their life-giving power (and vice versa).

Everyone needs alone time, especially in a relationship. To maintain a healthy bond, you must cherish your partner's personal space, and hold space for yourself. Each of you must remain focused on yourselves, and support each other with this potent need. You must give your partner space to do their "thing," and you must have space to do yours. Without our own paths and goals, we cease to be who we are. You must maintain your unique nature, or you will not be happy. If you are not happy alone, how on earth could you expect a relationship to work, or your communication to be fluid and enjoyable?

Whatever is happening inside you will be reflected outside of you. So, if you are battling through conversations with everybody, maybe it's time to reflect on what's happening inside…

Check in Often

In any healthy relationship, it is vital to check in with each other every so often to find out how both partners are feeling, both within themselves and within the relationship. There is nothing to fear here, but if you do not check in with each other often enough, the buildup of fear or resentment will stop the sharing and openness altogether—a recipe for disaster. Grievances must *always* be shared, and ideally, the partnership would create a relaxing, open space for this to occur…. how about December 23rd? (haha)

While it's hard to hear what the other person has to say about you or to discuss issues in your relationship, this is the most important opportunity for growth, both personally and together as a couple. This process will build a deeper trust between the two of you, so that when you face trying times, you will be ready to weather the storm.

Contemplations

- What was your biggest and most useful wake-up call after being in a "hot and heavy" relationship that went south?
- What fears have you conquered because of someone you developed a deep passion for?
- What is one excellent thing you can commit to doing right now for you and only you? What can you do to love yourself a little more?
- Parents and future parents: what is one way you can help your child(ren) harness their most exciting passion of the moment? What can you do to allow them to more fully express the things they are so excited to express?
- Do you love yourself *unconditionally*? Do you put heavy burdens on yourself that prevent you from having this unconditional feeling?
- What is one goal you and your partner can work on together for fun and for growth?
- What is one personal goal you've been putting to the side

that you would like to see come to fruition? What can you do today to get it moving?

6

Heartbreak

Heartbreak serves as an excellent way to achieve greater self-awareness. The heart might always undergo some sort of wounding when we part with loved ones, but the heart only breaks when we try to cling to someone's love or to the expectations in our heads about how they would forever in this life be with us.

Heartbreak brings pain in an exquisite fashion that cannot easily be put into words. It is like a thresher tearing through flesh and doesn't take back the damage it leaves in its path. There is no visible blood or wound, but the pain is real. It's indescribable, and what's more, it exists on a level that cannot be seen with the physical eyes. This creates a conundrum for the brain, as it cannot send signals to heal this sort of pain. It leaves you feeling war torn in ways which you must deal with *alone*.

Heartbreak may cause a man to question his entire existence. What is the point of life if you have no one to love or to be loved by? To achieve true love, in the romantic sense, is a beautiful and fulfilling accomplishment—and sometimes can feel like the only thing worth living for on this planet.

Self-Reflection

In the heart-broken moments you feel lost and alone, you may watch your life go up in flames and disappear like a puff of smoke. When you feel there's nothing left to give, and yet what you offered in your last relationship was never enough to make it work, it's time to look within to get to know yourself a little more.

What seems to be missing? It's important to find out, because everything happening outside of you is a mere reflection of what's going on inside your heart. Are there things you've been ignoring about yourself—feelings of inadequacy, jealousy, shame, guilt, or rejection? Don't ignore these red flags—they are there to guide you in a better direction.

If you are forced to learn a lesson the hard way, you may find comfort in knowing that your experience was probably so encompassing, you'll never need to learn that lesson again. The hardest lessons are often those that are avoided or ignored, and if you ignore lessons for long enough, the resulting pain will be that much more excruciating. This is why self-refection is so beneficial. Once you are comfortable exploring yourself and are no longer afraid of what you might find, the hard lessons will diminish into gentle suggestions within your everyday life.

Heartbreak is one of the most intimate sufferings you may endure, for after being so close with another person, they become a little part of you. They become part of your home, and because home is such a cherished place of safety and rest, it is a travesty to find your home destroyed by what was going on inside your head. Was it the other person who broke your heart, or was it you, yourself, replaying unhealthy trauma patterns from childhood? Or were you clinging to an outcome that no longer matched what your partner wanted?

Why does it hurt so much? What is the root of this pain? Is it the fear of losing something we hold dear? Or is it our clinging? When the heart clings to the energy of another, when they choose to pull away, you do indeed hurt your own heart by your clinging—by your fear to let go.

> *"If you love it, let it go."*

We might take comfort in remembering that we cannot escape our fate, so if something is meant for us, we will have it, even if it is not in the time frame we *think* is appropriate (or in the physical form we think is perfect). Fears of lack and failure often cause inner turmoil—fears of missing out. Be careful not to cling to anything (within the mind or the external world), because *everything* moves along. The more you resist change, the more pain you will face. Once you let the changes flow, you will witness something better than you can imagine come into your life... so long as you don't cling to your desires or your ideas of how things "should" go.

* * *

Heartbreak is so interesting in the way it can happen unexpectedly by events in your life that you never expected would have such an impact on your peace of mind. Fractures may be caused when your smoking-hot friend finds a lover (no big deal, no big deal...). Some of your scars might rupture when your ex pretends to care about you, and then disappears again, only to reappear a couple months later within the same old repeating pattern.

We can try to lie to ourselves and say these things don't hurt, but by denying the Truth, we only cover up our festering wounds. That is how the heart becomes rotten, bitter, and stagnant. That is how we age faster than is necessary.

The heart longs to express the Truth of your reality regardless of how disgusted you are with it—regardless of how dark and depressing it looks right this minute. Once you accept things as they are, and feel them, grieve the death of your ideas about your life that were wrong (rather than trying to sweep dust under the rug or living in fantasies or irrational projections), *that* is when you will authentically and powerfully move forward.

> *Love yourself enough to face the truth, no matter how ugly it may be. That is one exit door out of the rat race and one step closer to real peace.*

* * *

Pain is not enjoyable, but it is the best indication that growth is underway. While pain can be gruesome at some stages of this game, remember how much greater you're becoming.

We can work with relationship counselors to dig deeper into ourselves and to work out our problems. If they're good, they will ask questions to help us see ourselves more clearly, because *that* is what clears up those pesky relationship problems. In time, we may find that our relationship difficulties were not because of another person's flaws or inadequacy, but instead were caused by our own self-loathing thoughts and feelings, and because we perhaps deemed ourselves unworthy.

In order to have the most fulfilling and desirable relationship with another person, you must achieve happiness and true love within. This is a lifelong journey, so don't feel you've fallen behind or are inadequate in any way. You are worthy now, but you must learn to accept this Truth deeply. This is the path of self-forgiveness.

Greater Purpose

If you have been through a ridiculous amount of heartbreak, in part it is because you desire to have a deeply satisfying partnership. Achieving the self-awareness you need for that has required ample training. Now that you have it, you are more prepared to build a solid foundation with someone who is equally determined to bond deeply with you.

You will feel better about your situation soon. Do not worry. Everything is as it should be, even if you feel sad about the way things appear from your limited viewpoint. You have not wasted time—there is no such thing. Time is a tool, and everything you have done up to this point has served a purpose. If you feel you have wasted time, remember only *you* can stand in the way of achieving your goals.

Do not become bound by your circumstances. Move with the grace and ease of a Queen, and you will attract the King you desire (or vice versa) like a magnet. Centeredness and a willingness to remain in the flow are key components to your mastery of love. You want to be cherished and you will be.

But you must cherish yourself, so you attract those feelings from another. Use this as a refinement period in which you are calibrating ever-closer to your life partner.

Time Alone

Being alone is often thought of in a negative light, as if it isn't "right." It can be fun, but it can be dreadful, too. The truth is, no one is ever alone. You may access a sense of Oneness when you are fully grounded in your body. If you choose not to look within, are you choosing a life of isolation and loneliness, to perpetuate a story created by your ego?

Being without a life partner can be challenging. Not having that familiar energy close by, especially on all of those cold nights… that part is not fun. However, this temporary period is necessary for great healing and total transformation, if you desire such. Make use of the time, discover yourself at a deeper level, discover your uniqueness. Become rooted in your existence and purpose. This inner work will never be complete, and only gets sweeter the longer you eat!

If you work on yourself every day, your awareness will continuously reach new heights, and you will come ever-closer to feeling *free*. Every day is an opportunity to develop better habits and treat yourself as royalty, which will shift your life in magical ways very rapidly. Listen to your intuition and do not doubt yourself. Know that you are prepared to welcome the person with whom you desire to share your life.

Become centered, with and without someone by your side, and you cannot fail. Be the best person you can count on—nothing feels more secure than that. Do not be afraid to continue on the road less followed, for that is the road courageous leaders aim for, no matter the thoughts and words of others. You may feel you're on your own in this, but again, you are never alone. You are on a noble mission to seek the light within, to heal past pains and experience Oneness on the physical plane. Breathe deeply. Exhale fully. Remain present and you will see perfection unfold around you. Your heart will be content in no time.

> *Take two steps forward and one step back to develop a foundation that will never crack.*

The Power of Surprise

It's hard to wait, whether for your dream relationship or for your "dreams coming true." It's especially challenging not knowing what's coming next, but on the other hand, isn't the unknown, the element of surprise, part of the fun? If you knew everything that was coming, wouldn't that eliminate the potency and excitement of your curiosity? Maintain confidence and patience during these times of change. Follow Universal Law and do breathing exercises during the day. Conscious breathing alone can have a tremendous impact on your progress toward happiness and attracting your perfect partner.

How to Heal

It can be a challenge to be between romantic relationships. You may begin to long for your ex-partner, but in these moments of weakness, do your best to remember that true love requires no undesirable compromises or silly games, or any infringement upon your freedom of expression.

Harness the transformational potential of any pain you experience and use it to your advantage. There is vast power here you can amplify and direct to further your goals and bring them closer to fruition. Believe you will receive the results you desire, and you will. "Thy will be done" is Universal Law, after all.

Treat yourself as a Queen (or King), and others will admire you, and your King (or Queen) will treat you with the respect you deserve. It is a privilege for anyone to enter your Kingdom, just as it is an honor for you to be invited into someone else's Kingdom. Remembering this will help you feel reverence for *every* moment of life, with or without a partner by your side.

You are doing well and learning things that will make you stronger. The experience of heartbreak is a potent time to reshape the masterpiece of yourself and your life. Use this opportunity to grow and be better than you ever thought possible. Remember to:

- Monitor your thought patterns—you *must* be happy within to find happiness without.
- Release your tears and sorrow—better to let it out than let it sink in and rot. But do not wallow in excess, for lingering in misery can become detrimental to your health and happiness.
- Build yourself up with whatever you need to feel *worthy* (because you are, and if you don't see it, you must uncloud your vision).
- Learn the art of expression, so you may more easily convey

your needs and feelings to another, and so you can perceive their needs more accurately.
- Do not be afraid to be open, as the more open you are, the smoother things will flow in all areas of your life.
- Do your best not to create expectations for they can cause you to close yourself off to the endless flow of possibilities!

Process any deep-seated feelings of guilt or shame by understanding their true essence, which includes not facing your True Self at a deep enough level. The easiest way to do this is through the Daily Work. Commune within to find the answers you seek. Answers will come when you're prepared to receive them.

To avoid unnecessary regrets, you must be patient and act with conscious awareness. To feel better about yourself, align with your most exciting goals. Let your light shine bright, and nothing will stand in the way of your freedom and happiness. Let intuition guide you to true love. Then it will be smooth sailing.

Inner Security

As a woman, it's hard to figure out what a man's intentions are if he is unsure what is "right" for him. You may experience mixed signals. How interested in you is he?

This can make a woman's life stressful, for she might count on the certainty of her man for her own security. This may stem from basic survival instincts, and there is nothing *wrong* with this. But, once you have identified this as an issue in your life, recognize that you have the power to build a sense of security within yourself. Take charge of how you feel. You are not a victim, but rather a powerful Light Being placed on this planet to express your truest essence for your enjoyment and expansionary benefit, and to make the world around you a better place. What a purpose!

If you feel powerless over a situation that has occurred in your relationship, take it as an opportunity to build yourself from the *inside* out. You are not flawed. You are perfection in the process of manifesting.

Take heartbreak as a wake-up call. Behave rationally. Learn to trust yourself. Do not put your trust in things or people not aligned with you. You have everything you need within you to succeed and to feel fulfilled. You do not need a life partner for these things. Release the belief that you need something outside of you to fill holes that only *you* can fill. A life partner is a welcome addition to life, yes—the delicious topping for the masterpiece dessert you're creating within. Once you realize this, everything you desire will flow into your life. That will be the time your partner comes forth. Do not rely on exterior experiences for your happiness. That is the road to disappointment and regret.

If you are experiencing lack or emptiness, it is because you are closing yourself off from All That Is. Just know, activities like shopping or excessive partying will not solve this feeling. That will not fill the void. Set yourself a beautiful, exciting goal, remain open to the flow, and be ready for greater things (beyond your current imaginative capability).

Restore a Relationship

Restoring a relationship is a process, but can be done with the right words and actions which flow instantly from within if you remain open, focus on your heart center, and *accept* the present moment as it is. Remember to:

- Behave with honor and respect for *all* Beings at all times, no matter your perception or preconceived opinions.
- Be open to positive change in *all* people, no matter the dictations or beliefs of your ego.
- Focus on peace and harmony while communicating with others, especially when egos are triggered.
- Focus on gratitude and remaining centered in your day-to-day life and your inner wisdom will come through more clearly.

A relationship can only be restored when both sides of the damaged bond have a desire to restore it. By your genuine acceptance of the present moment as it is, you stop clinging to your desired outcome, which gives the bond a better chance to heal. Think of the bond as a river of energy. If you create a dam or small little channel where you *think* the energy should flow, you are effectively blocking off the infinitely better ways that exist for you and the other person to bond together.

Take Care of Stagnant Energy

When neither party has direction or clarity, relationships can get bogged down by stagnant energy. They've forgotten who they are as individuals, and while they may love each other, they've lost the magic and do not know what to do next. It is possible to turn these situations around, provided that both parties are committed, first to themselves, and then to the relationship. Each person must explore themselves as individuals once again and rediscover what makes them excited to live. Make goals and achieve them—first individually, then as a couple. You could see the cobwebs vanish overnight!

Remain true to yourself, for that will ensure your happiness, no matter what happens in your relationship or in your life. If you are ever to have a harmonious, fulfilling bond with someone of equal caliber, you must become autonomous.

* * *

If you cannot answer the question "Why are you here?" with certainty and excitement, you have important foundational work to do, before you can get to the more exciting work of *doing* the things you set out to do.

You are on an epic journey, filled with unlimited potential and surprises. You are heading in the right direction, even if you feel lost or depressed sometimes. Do not worry. Everything works out for your greatest good. Do your best with the Daily Work and remember the breath. The goal is to always be present and focused. You are on the verge of something incredible. Don't stop now!

> *Behave with dignity, show honor and courage in all you do, and you will fly through life unscathed by the shallow shortcomings of those who choose not to live up to the high moral standards of Universal Law.*

Contemplations

- Have you ever felt inadequate, either in your relationships or in other situations in life?
- Can you pinpoint why you felt this way?
- Is there something about other people that triggers your jealousy? This could be signaling something for you to work on.
- Can you pinpoint a common pattern or thread through all of your romantic relationships that have ended?
- Did something from your childhood cause you to think negatively about yourself?
- Are there people in your life about whom you hold a negative opinion? What could you do to keep your expectations at bay each time you encounter them?
- Are you dependent on any of your relationships for your happiness or fulfillment? What is one way you can become more autonomous?

7

Failure

Failure is another type of experience that may cause you to reexamine your purpose in life, whether that be failure in a job, failure in love, in friendship, or in understanding yourself. These reexamination periods are a critical junction point in your self-awareness journey.

The moments you feel stuck are good indicators that you are not moving in a beneficial direction, or that you're carrying with you too much resistance. The moments there seem to be obstacles at every turn and nothing goes your way are times in life you must relax and observe your path from a different perspective. Your brain may simply be stuck in its old ways and perhaps you have outgrown them. The obstacles and failures are there to nudge you to look from a different angle.

Failure doesn't feel good because maybe we think we did everything we could to make something work the way we thought it should, and yet, the flow continued on in its own way regardless of our expectations, so something had to give way. Your failures can feel better if you use them as signaling tools that indicate your higher self sees something better for you, and when you think about all the effort and time that may feel wasted, just know, nothing you experience is ever a waste. It is all good information you can use to get to know yourself better, and that is the point after all.

What is failure, really? We could say that failure is, in all actuality, a label created by the brain using a small set of information hand picked by the ego for self-deprecation. In Reality, failure is not a useful label or concept since *everything* that occurs in this time-space plane is useful information to help guide us in our Soul Mission, down the ancient road Home, to comprehend the flow and learn to ride the wave with some skill. All of life's events are teaching us to drive at the cosmic level, to integrate the fifth dimension, to comprehend the Great Upheaval or transition period this world is coming into.

Failure, a concept nailed into our undeveloped brains in early childhood, is now a mechanism which holds our attention within the excessive static in our energy field. This makes it more challenging to move forward in our self-awareness journey as we insist on self-hatred and reviving grudges against ourselves, creating a mess of "groundhog days". This decision to hate ourselves for our "failures" allows our brain to hold us in a hamster wheel, or more accurately stated, the all-famous Rat Race. But, you are not a victim of your brain. This is something you can wake up from and begin controlling your game to make life the way you want it to be as the Great Creator you are becoming, or rather, remembering.

This is enlightenment at its finest. Wring each failure experience for everything it's worth. Honor it, appreciate it, bask in the Knowing that you are becoming the best version of yourself. You can take the lessons now or leave them for the next round—it is always your choice.

Ego Death

Failure may come with severe pains, including ego death—rather unenjoyable, but essential if one desires to continue sculpting or pruning the greatest creation yet, which is indeed the ego. No one can have an over-inflated ego —an unkempt garden— and do well in a more powerful state—your energy field would be very unstable. Once you think you are better than another person in any capacity, you become dangerous to yourself and all of humanity. The Universe and Karma have ways of dealing with actions that stem from these lines of thought, to maintain the pristine quality of the Kingdom within—the Inner Garden.

The other side of the over-inflated ego is self-deprecation and feeling unworthy—feeling as if people (any person) is better than you. You must become aware of these belief systems, both when you find yourself standing on a pedestal looking down on another, and when you look up at others as you place them on pedestals above you. This requires sensitivity to what you have going on inside at every moment—noticing where you are identifying with your ego's limited vision of reality. Be humble but remember who you are (royalty) to regain your natural confidence so you can lead your Kingdom and anyone who desires to follow a capable, clear-sighted leader.

Greater Purpose

If you ever sit down to consider all the experiences you've labeled as failures in your life, it is beneficial to think on each one for a while and analyze *why* you have labeled them as such. Each failure you go through has a noble purpose to teach you a lesson about your life and your direction. It is up to you to figure out what the lesson is and learn from it. If you can pinpoint what went "wrong" by your own standards, that understanding is the success that matters—and maybe you will not have to repeat the experience! Self-evaluation can be uncomfortable and even painful, but if you do it, you will go much further in your journey here. The road is not always paved smooth, so bear this in mind when you do not see the next move or turn in the path. The road will become clear at the right time. But, the sooner you can offer yourself some forgiveness, the faster you will be able to move on.

Certainty is critical in executing every action with precision. Remember, you will have all the answers you need as you learn to trust yourself. Do not waste time fretting over the past, for you have freedom now to view or do things differently. If something is outside your reach to change, then perhaps it is not for you to change. But you always retain the power to *change your focus*. That is the magnificence of each unique Creator born onto this planet. You are more prepared for the future than you realize. Do not question the masterpiece unfolding, even if it doesn't make sense at the moment—it will in due time.

> *The movement toward a goal is where satisfaction and fulfillment may be found.*

The Public School System

Failure is a useful tool for honing skills or for nudging one back onto their Path if they've lost their way. So, let us say something doesn't go according to plan... is that "failure", or is that us getting attached to our expectations and not wanting to accept how things ended up? Either way, it is all valuable information, so there is nothing *wrong* with "failure", and nothing to be ashamed of whatsoever. Thus, it is a crime against humanity to have schools set up in the catastrophic manner in which they are set up, whereby failure becomes a red mark on a young child's heart, a point of embarrassment, and a point of dread and hatred toward the Self. It is not beneficial in any capacity and causes long-term mental and emotional scarring, lasting into adulthood and perhaps even onto the death bed.

How could any institution as large and powerful as any major public school system be so misguided in logic? A country such as the United States is supposed to uphold freedom of being, and yet look at what it is doing to the light of the country: smothering it where it begins, in the beginning...

Schools should not feel like manufacturing facilities. Children are creative and carefree, and should not be taught that failure makes them *unworthy*. It is better to send children to small schools run by people who have a say in what goes on with the curriculum. It is better to give good teachers more freedom to choose how to best teach each individual child, for all children are unique and must be taught to develop this uniqueness, rather than how to conform to the masses. Large public education institutions have too many layers of bureaucracy and administrative complication, causing administrators to be too far removed from the reality that is the children's everyday experience.

The Great Journey

This is your journey of Life. What are you making of it? Breathtaking masterpieces? Or dull mediocrity that you're not really proud of? Keep in mind that a masterpiece can take many forms, and we might not fairly judge which is better or worse from this limited perspective. A masterpiece can be as sweet as a homemade birthday card for mommy, or as tragic as a love affair gone astray. A perfect latte for yourself on a Sunday, or an awkward first kiss in a driveway. Your first heartbreak, your second heartbreak, who you became after the pain finally faded away. Even after concocting what appears to be failure after failure, what you are really doing is crafting and sculpting the greatest masterpiece of them all, which is you, manifested in physical form.

So, as you can see, there is nothing to fear. Existence is never-ending, so no event may be fairly singled out as one complete failure. Every piece of this matrix is part of your masterpiece. Every piece matters, whether you see that now, or ten years from now. The worst thing you can do is beat yourself up over past mistakes. The worst sin you can commit is to treat yourself with disrespect. Determine what respect means for you, and learn to treat yourself as royalty, for that is what you are. You are the only one who can stand in your way to success and achieving the goals you have set for yourself.

Again, you mustn't regret things of the past, for they have served an important role in your expansion experience. Keep your heart and mind open to the endless possibilities and you will not be disappointed. Do not forget why you have chosen to be here in the first place: to light the torches of the world. You will succeed. You are here to make a grand impact, and you shall, in the right time-space. For now, you prepare and move forward stronger than ever before—you have it within you, so do it!

If you are stubborn and fail because of your reluctance to go with the flow, remember that change makes progress possible. Without change, there would be no existence in time-space, which is itself manifested out of and by change – the Great Flower Blossoming.

Remember, too: no one may do you harm unless you allow it to occur, even if you are unaware of your allowing (i.e. leaky boundaries). This is why it is critical to realize your destructive thought patterns and change them. They are the source of any suffering you've endured. You have it in your power now to make the changes you've been waiting for. The question is: are you willing to accept the challenge and take responsibility for your own well-being? Or are you willing, like many people, to put that responsibility and power into the hands of anyone who would like to take it from you? Choose whatever course is best for you. You are the Divine Creator, here to unleash the greatness you have bottled up inside. Do not deprive the world of your exquisite unique factor!

It is of critical importance that you learn to harness your inner strength and courage, for this will carry you forward into the darkness, which you will bring to light. It is not always a smooth path, but you will find your way if you listen to the voice within without hesitation.

You are brave and bold in your own unique way, and that is admirable. Continue developing your skills and building yourself, and you will thrive, no matter what is happening around you.

Contemplations

- What is your most recent failure? Why do you consider it as such?
- What is one lesson you took from it?
- In what way is it nudging you in a more beneficial direction?
- For parents: if your child(ren) attends a traditional school, is there a way you can soften their perception of failure, so they may look at their wrong answers more objectively and not as points of embarrassment, unworthiness, or insecurity?
- Do you repeat negative thoughts about yourself that stem from failure and/or childhood? Identify them, write them down, and, one at a time, eliminate them. This can be done by manually replacing these thoughts (as soon as you notice yourself thinking them) with a better thought about yourself. If you find childhood memories that still haunt you or make you *feel* any sort of way, take some time and give your child self the love he or she needed in that traumatic moment. These memories may seem silly today, but for a child, they were highly impactful and scarring. Let yourself feel the unprocessed emotions to once and for all release them. Caring for your child self as if they were

here with you now can be quite powerful and healing.

8

Death

The topic of death is heavy, but it needn't come with such an overload of baggage or misery. "Death" also does not need to refer to death of the physical form, for as you may discover later in your path, death does not *need* to occur in the physical body unless you choose that self-destructive path....[3] The more we cling to our beliefs of reality, the more we will prove to ourselves that we are right—hence the concept of "groundhog day".

Types of Death

Spiritual, emotional, and mental deaths occur throughout our lives, and allow us to be reborn: the death of an old way of thinking makes way for something new and more profound. A time of redecorating, no matter how trivial it may appear, may express an inner transformation underway. Out with the

---

[3] See Harold Waldwin Percival, *Thinking and Destiny* (New York: The Word Foundation, Inc., 2006).

old, in with the new, as they say! Spiritual death may occur many times as you explore and accept Inner Truth. Emotional death is quite apparent as you navigate your relationships with others.

Death is a spring cleaning of the soul, a critical piece of the puzzle of Life, and we may venture to guess you do indeed enjoy the feeling of being reborn. Death may be seen as the energetic removal of an outgrown perspective from your past, to make way for your next level of openness. If you did not remove old, stagnant items within your mind and soul, they would fester and rot, leading to your demise, in one form or another. Do not be surprised if death comes with pain and aggravation, as these are signals that part of your Soul (which you have likely neglected over the years) has stagnated, or you are resisting the release of your expectations or beliefs. Time to check in....

Physical Death

While experiences like failure and heartbreak may reach deep into your psyche, causing you to reexamine your whole purpose for being, the death of a loved one is a beast of another caliber. It will make you throw down *everything* you thought you knew about yourself, about life, about things you thought were important.

Death is a brutal, unforgiving dark lord of the night, but he serves a most worthy task in the fight for the mind. When death strikes one person down, others perk up and wonder, *what went wrong*? After all, this is supposed to be the Garden of Life... What are we missing? Is it simply... simplicity? When we go back to the topic of the brain and think about its tendency to complicate everything, death comes as a rude, but useful, awakening to help us more clearly see our tunnel vision of reality. Death makes us notice what is worth keeping and what is totally unnecessary. When we realize we've spent too much time thinking and nit picking petty little things, the death of a loved one can be a sharp reminder that maybe we're not focusing on our masterpiece.

> *Face the pain and then let it out. If you do not, others around you will suffer the side effects of your unprocessed trauma.*

Take time to heal from your loss. Nurture yourself. Find your passion and live it better than you did before. Let your loss become a beautiful fire in your soul. Create something great in the memory of your beloved. Make something you Know they would be proud of. Channel your love for them back into this world.

Heart-Brain Connection

To face the great pain death brings is equivalent to a young knight facing and harnessing the great dragon of the heart and soul, to conquer the dark shadows of the mind (i.e. death of the ego). The heart center holds the wisdom of all of time; the mind must be conquered and trained, or you will face your own demise. In other words, the mind, if left to rule the roost, will create a false you, a version of yourself which is not based in Truth. The heart must be recognized as your driver's seat, so to speak, as this is the only way the light of your awareness can reach all the corners of your Being, to remove all darkness, unworthiness, unforgiveness.

The internal dragon protects the treasure, which is this driver's seat or throne - the place where once you come upon it, it can affect the entire world. When you become fully aware that you are protected no matter where you are in the physical world, you will be in a more optimal position to express yourself without those pesky fears, most of which boil down to the fear of death. To achieve this level of security, use the Daily Work.

Is this the Holy (Whole-y) Trinity: The heart being put back into command, the brain (and body) being used to manifest, and a strong, clear connection between them being the key to infinite abundance of love, resources, and happiness? What if all we must do to see our world perfected is focus our attention on redeveloping our heart-brain connection, and learning to use the brain to translate what the heart wants us to create?

To achieve this great state requires all shadows within to be burned away, to reveal the True Self within, like the Great Phoenix Rising. The ego is not evil, but your unconsciousness of it is clear evidence that the brain has been running the show to the point where it has created a web of delusional images of the Self based, not on Truth, but on the past, based on unneeded and excessive self-protection. It is high time we shake off those cobwebs and come back into the present moment, allowing all erroneous ideologies to be shed as we make our way into a new era of peace and true, fulfilling happiness…

Inner Strength

The more deaths (of any kind) you experience, the more robust you become. The inner strength you gain access to as a result of enduring grief or a traumatic experience is something to be proud of, yet not something to take for granted.

As each experience comes with growing pains and a shedding of old ways, do your best to remember the emotional depths you were drawn to. Every death can be seen and used as your own private well of wisdom, so that you may continue to harness the power of each one for many years to come. As you develop your inner vision and are able to maintain a cleaner perspective, you will be able to bypass most pain. Pain is simply resistance to the inevitable Unfolding.

So, it is often best, and the least ungrounding, to be as openhearted, confident, and courageous as you can be, so you may look back on each death experience and know you used it to its fullest capacity for growth and transformation. Wring it for everything it's worth. This is your life. Make it count.

> *Life is a gift. Don't waste even a single day doing things you don't enjoy. Cherish every moment as if it were your last, for it very well could be.*

Do not be fooled by all the external shenanigans that distract you from accomplishing your divine work, which is to understand yourself and perceive Truth, so you may share it with your greatest companions, who may then share it with theirs, until it spreads like wildfire. While wildfire may cause damage in its wake, what comes after is a renewed living environment for all of nature to thrive in, better than before. Death is sometimes needed for new life to more easily spring forth.

Unasked Questions

There are certain aspects of physical death that are quite sensitive and so are not discussed. For example, *should* we feel mournful when someone passes? What if someone doesn't feel this sorrow? Does that make them insensitive or a psychopath? Or does it mean they are maintaining their broader, wiser perspective on the totality of Life, and they've realized that Life never ends, but instead *transforms* to the next phase of existence? Does a lack of grief mean they understand that the Being that has "passed away" is still right here where they have always been, that it is possible to communicate with them, and that communication doesn't require things like a physical mouth or black magic? If we continue covering up these types of questions, and instead continue on with our mournful, depressing worship of the dead, what will become of these important understandings? Will they become festering wounds buried deep inside, unasked and unanswered? You will cause destruction to yourself if you lack courage to bring these questions to light, looking any fear of rejection straight in the face and seeing it for what it is: an illusion created by the brain.

Illusions of the Brain

Illusions are ninety percent of what you perceive of this world, which is the problem at present. Most fears are illusions too, including the fear of death. You must look within to see Truth, to see what you're missing, to gain perspective on reality as it is—not how you *think* it is. This is not a joke. It is critical that all human beings on this planet understand this concept of illusion versus reality, because when fear rules the world, nothing substantial gets done, wars pop up, everything stagnates—including people—and depression runs rampant. Sound familiar?

People are stubborn and set in their ways, all because of the desire to follow the herd and because of the over-functioning of the brain. The brain is the original AI gone awry—but not if you wake up and use it as it was designed: to conceptualize your unique desires which you collect from within the Heart Center, to manifest into the physical at your whim. It is not more complicated than it sounds, but the brain needs to be redirected for this to work as intended. *You can do this.*

Death assists you in coming back to how things *are*. It provides a massive shift in perspective when you're attached to too many things outside of yourself. You are not bound to anything on this planet, yet you choose to remain within this perspective, suffering as you *choose* to do, when death occurs or when you imagine what will happen when you lose this house, or that car, or that relationship, or that job… Why?

Even if your physical reality does not match your ideal, it is coming. Allow yourself to focus on what you want, no matter what. All suffering is optional. Much can change in a year, a week, even in one day. You must trust The Way, for it is unfolding perfectly, as it always has and always will, no matter what you think. Follow your gut instinct and *explore* your pain (do not suppress it) to understand why it is there so that you may finally move on peacefully.

Have mercy on your soul and be kind to yourself, for in the end, you are all you have.

Contemplations

- How has the death of a loved one helped you gain valuable perspective on your life?
- What did it cause you to focus on more clearly? What did it cause you to break away from—bad habits, a job, an undesirable group of friends?
- Do you fear death? Most people do. The question is, "*Why?*"
- Do you fear big changes in life? The next time you're faced with one, try practicing broadening your perspective. What is the root of the fear?
- Parents: What are some ways you can teach your child(ren) to broaden their untrained perspective when faced with challenging situations? This skill will carry them through life.

9

Manipulation

Manipulation is a sneaky game that everyone uses at one point or another—sometimes for innocent tasks, at other times for nasty plans. This is why the ability to read people is imperative, so you can read past their words and discover their true motives, to determine their purity or perhaps their filth!

People use manipulation in many situations—from the dishonest sales agent to the narcissist convincing a will-maker to put everything into their name, to the four-year-old telling mommy all the reasons ice cream is needed right away. To remain balanced—and if you want everyone to have what they want—do the Daily Work. Check-in with yourself daily and you will keep a firm grasp of what is right and just, for you and everyone you influence.

Do your best to keep your own needs and desires in mind (as well as those of others you encounter). There is no need for self-sacrifice. Once you self-sacrifice once, you are more likely to do it again. Then your self-respect will diminish, others will treat you less respectfully, and you may become a bigger target for manipulation.

Keep an eye out for bad energy and intentions, for some people are not in an abundance mindset. These people are not "wrong" or "evil;" they just don't see clearly. You can show them a better way, and they will probably appreciate it (someday). Giving someone a bad deal never has good energy around it for anyone involved.

Manipulators

A manipulator desires a particular outcome and hopes to control the targeted manipulated individual(s) so their own vision manifests. Sometimes the manipulator does this with tunnel vision (meaning they don't see a better way, or they really think their way is the only or best way), and sometimes the manipulator enjoys being the cat playing with a mouse. In either case, they disregard the resistance they create in the lives of those they are manipulating with their blatant desire to control.

If you are a manipulator, even if in just a few situations, remember your limited perspective. Things will flow as they flow, and will continue to do so, with or without your control. It is relaxing, you will find, to let things go and see how they pan out. This way, all those involved may learn the lessons they came to this planet to learn and experience firsthand. It is best *not* to interfere, as your interference can be a detriment to your well-being, humanity, and the rest of existence (resistance has a ripple effect). It is also not always your job to deny someone else an important learning experience by you taking over to "help" when they didn't want it.

The Manipulated

If you have been manipulated to the detriment of your own goals and well-being, take this opportunity to notice and end that phase of your life. Promise yourself from here on to be more aware of your surroundings, on both the physical and energetic levels. This way, you will always know (as deeply as you can) someone else's intentions. If someone is up to no good, you will feel it. You will see it in their eyes. There is no hiding when you know what to look for. Develop eyes to see and ears to hear, if only to protect your own well-being and your ability to create freely.

Become as wise as a serpent. Maintain a keen sense of your instinct, for it never lies. Do not make false accusations but be wary of strange behaviors. Don't be afraid to ask questions where they might be warranted.

It is easier to manipulate someone who has a passive disposition. If this is your tendency, learn to be assertive. Stand your ground, set your boundaries, learn what you need to do in order to feel respected by others, and feel confident in protecting your right to be here. People will treat you the way you allow them to treat you. Sometimes people you encounter behave like children, always testing their limits. Show them clear boundaries, and you will have their respect quickly. Then they will be less likely to manipulate you… or at least it won't be so easy to do.

Manipulation for Control

There is a fine line between maintaining a respectful level of control and developing a desire for excessive, tyrant-like levels of control. You must discover within yourself *exactly* where to draw the line in any given situation (business, politics, religion), because this can be a slippery slope for some people's minds.

Sometimes it takes an intervention, and sometimes it requires tragedy, to reestablish those ever-important checks and balances on your concept of reality, and to gain perspective on what is working and what is creeping up on "dysfunctional" or "unhealthy". Doing the Daily Work helps keep everything in line, allowing you to maintain clarity on what you should and should not control each day. Remember to listen to the voice within, for it knows what decision will serve you best.

Instead of trying to control a situation, especially if your desire to control comes from your insecurities, letting go and going with the flow provides the greatest outcome for most situations, with a fun element of surprise added for texture! Things do not have to pan out as you have them in your head. You do not need to know everything that will happen at every moment. Take each day step-by-step. You will be amazed at what your brilliant mind and soul can create when you relax and enjoy whatever happens.

Remember, your life is your masterpiece! Cherish each second like a painter cherishes each brushstroke: with conscious awareness, a steady hand, and a gentle touch. The result may look different (but maybe better) than what you expected or intended.

Justice

Justice comprises the internal rules that govern existence as it *truly* is, not as how you think it is. Justice has always and will always reign, for it is inherent within the frequency-based design we are living in. While some aspects of our physical reality may appear to run amuck without justice being present at all, there is still the innate Knowing of justice we each hold within us. Even if someone commits a wrongdoing, it will sit with them for all of eternity until it is corrected, or gets infected. They will have their "day in court," whether on this planet or in a more subtle form. The subtleties that occur within each person often teach the deepest lessons. For when one Being commits a crime against another, that frequency will sit within them somewhere, like a grain of sand, irritating them until a lesson is learned the hard way, such as by manifesting into a life-threatening disease, an accident, or attracting similar behavior from another person.

Justice is one fail-safe of this divine design, for without it, existence as we know it would cease to exist. No matter how hard the human race tries to remove this critical piece of this reality puzzle, they cannot. Energy speaks for itself.

Justice may be thought of as the Oval Office within your soul (perhaps more accurately, the Noble Office). This includes both serving justice to others and doing right by yourself. When you live a just life, you must include yourself in the justice you serve, so that you walk your talk (no matter how much your ego might want to say one thing and do another).

To travel further on your inner path, you must right all your wrongs, no matter how embarrassing or dreadful it may feel. It is always more important to uphold Truth and justice than to entertain your ego. You will become more centered, relaxed, and many health problems may fade on their own. So, for anyone to have and maintain a clear conscience, heart, and soul, justice *must* be served. This way, the physical body too may be cleansed and healed forever.

Morality

Morality serves as the justification for *why* every nasty action you've committed is just that: nasty. Why would you call it such if you didn't have a reason to? The reason is *morality*. Most people were raised knowing and living by the basic morals, and the core of these morals is Truth, which is indeed built into the DNA—we feel it within and cannot ignore it. Of course, you may *try* to ignore it, such as by blocking yourself from your heart and residing solely within your brain like a self-made prison, but any acts you commit that go against Truth will create guilt that will begin to fester and spread (and may even morph into cancer if you're not careful).

If you Know that what you're doing is not right for you, take a step back. Re-examine your actions from a broader, heart-centered perspective. What motivated you? What was the original drive? Most likely, it was not *bad*. Maybe you were just trying to fill a void inside yourself. Whatever your motivation was can be met through other means more aligned with who you are *now* and how you want to present yourself to the world.

As you move forward in any situation, keep track of these thoughts and feelings. Your actions must match or exceed your standards, or else you will degrade yourself and your perfect expression. Morality is the external manifestation of what we all know at the core of our Being, which is Truth, pure and simple. It cannot be changed or tainted.

Sometimes, something is done with a clear head and heart, and when you look back upon it, some other detail creeps up that perhaps wasn't noticed before. Perhaps as a child you would sneak booze or money or the car from your parents, so you could enjoy it with your friends. Maybe you cheated on a school test or shoplifted and later you realized this wasn't honest, and isn't something you would ever think of doing today. But have no fear! You have no reason to hate yourself for past decisions—you made them to the best of your ability, and self-loathing can cause very deep damage. This is the beauty of the self-awareness journey. Be glad you've evolved!

Contemplations

- When have you been a manipulator?
- What situations do you often feel the need to control? What is the root of this need – fear, insecurity, bad habit of not minding your own business? What happens if you let the control go?
- When was the last time someone manipulated you? Did you see it coming? Can you prevent it from happening again, peacefully?
- Can you identify areas in your life where you could create better boundaries for yourself regarding how others treat you (and how you treat yourself)?
- How often do you feel that intuitive "red flag" about someone or what they are saying? Do you listen to it or ignore it?

10

Temptation

If something provides immediate pleasure (a dopamine rush), with no obvious long-term benefit, potential long-term degradation of Self, and produces within you even a whiff of guilt or shame or embarrassment if someone caught you in the act, it is likely a temptation.

> As a wise man once said, "Don't take the short path because it's easy. Take the long road because it's hard."

Temptation has been discussed since biblical times, yet few have mastered the way around this challenging obstacle. While temptations change form, temptation's pull remains. It is up to you as the Creator to identify temptation and stop it in its tracks the moment it enters your pristine masterpiece of Life. Stop it as it enters your thoughts and emotions, and do not let it go any further than that (e.g. by letting it become a regrettable word or action).

After avoiding each temptation in your path, you may be

temporarily disappointed, but let us be clear here: this is your ego's disappointment, not Yours. This is you restructuring your neural networks, which takes effort and energy, especially when attempting to disrupt old, established bad habits. In the long run, if you deny the ego its temptations (such as a quick dopamine hit), you will accumulate the types of treasures that shall endure through this life and beyond, those which are scarcely imaginable without this self-dedication and Daily Work. This is the way to develop confidence, self-love, self-worth, honor, and fortitude, to see your purpose clearly, to become passionate about your goals, and to fully establish the all-important moral compass that will serve as your passport in this life and beyond.

Anyone may find themselves stranded in their own thoughts, caught between a tempting action and a more noble reaction. In this moment, you choose not only your specific direction but also the standards to which you will hold yourself moving forward. This decision has a trickle-down effect, whereby others with whom you interact will hold you to those same standards, and treat you accordingly. By this simple mechanism (the moment right before you decide which path you will take when faced with each temptation), you hold the power in your hands regarding how your life will play out.

If you choose the path of temptation, whatever form that may be in—bad habits, watching porn, cheating, gambling, lying, even giving in to an emotional trigger—you, in that instant, degrade your self-respect, self-worth, and self-trust. **You** delay your greatest life being made manifest.

Daily Habits Are Everything

While taking the high road may feel like a challenging or undesirable path, particularly when faced with your most compelling personal temptations or addictions, it is by far the better choice for your long-term perception of yourself. Each time you deny temptation, you build character. Choosing the path that feels "right" *to you* will give you something to be proud of - something meaningful to live for.

This struggle is a lifelong adventure, which may become easier over time and with experience. Some types of temptations will fade into nothingness, but you will always face new challenges. Do not beat yourself up if you find yourself slipping. Just be firm. Choose to do better next time—and then do better next time. Treat yourself with respect, no matter what you've done. You are here to learn and grow, and actions you label as "mistakes" are the most expansive experiences you will encounter.

Have mercy on yourself. You've heard this many times now, but it is imperative that you learn to love yourself enough to want to clean up your unproductive habits so that you may enjoy perfect mind and body health. As much as possible, you must be consciously aware of your behavior.

At this point in the world's history, many of the most important character traits (e.g. honesty, dependability, compassion, respect, etc.) have been swept under the rug and forgotten. This explains the downfall of societies all around the civilized world. Strong, virtuous leaders may still be found in remote tribes who live close to their roots, but these people are dwindling in number. If you want to become a better person, put fortitude and gratitude at the front of your mind, then take it one day at a time.

> *Enjoy the moments you have right in front of you, for therein lie all of your opportunities for betterment and growth.*

Identify and Release Triggers

Emotional triggers are tricky since they come with an instant release of hormones and a strong desire to lash out at whomever triggered you. Once you have the right level of inner motivation —when you know you have work to do that is more important than soothing your ego, proving yourself right, or proving someone else wrong— triggers become a thing of the past.

Thought and emotional patterns are developed in the brain at a young age, based on your environment and the people upon whom you are most dependent. You are influenced by the emotional patterns of your family (and anyone else who spends a great deal of time with you before adolescence, such as teachers). Without enough self-awareness to identify these patterns coming from the people around you as you grow up, you will likely adopt them as your own. But now as an adult you can identify unhealthy patterns, perceived limitations, emotional triggers and their destructive nature, so that you can move past the box they have created around you.

No one can steal the Truth within you. They can only attempt, with temptations and distractions, to make you forget or to cloud your inner vision.

Emotional Trigger Release Exercises

When faced with an emotional, trigger-happy situation:

- *Pause for a moment before responding.* Take a deep breath or two. Refocus on your heart center in that precious moment right when you feel "triggered." You have the power to change your external reality now, rather than responding (with your ego) immediately. That one moment is your opportunity to exit one part of your rat race.
- *Choose your responses carefully* to soften and release those triggers. This will improve the steadiness of your frequency and bring you closer to your center and goals.
- *Remember who you are and why you're here.* Regardless of your beliefs, you have a real purpose: to create excellence as the Great Creator you are, by no mistake. This purpose is far more important than lashing out at someone else's passing comment or action. What have you done with your precious time? What will you do next? Be particular—or at least make a plan.
- *Choose your battles wisely.* You do not see the full picture, even if you *think* you do. A good rule of thumb: if you feel like fighting, you *don't* understand the whole picture. Carry this with you throughout each day, and it may soften

(and eventually remove) those pesky triggers.

While it requires strength, ambition, and determination to choose your emotions (especially when you've begun your day in a bad mood), these are the moments to notice and shift, regardless of how your ego feels. It may help to think that anyone who is looking for a reaction from you is only doing so to take energy from you. Reacting is you giving them your precious resources in a dirty sort of way, but all is fair in an energy exchange! Just beware, they'll do it again if you reveal more of your leaky boundaries.

You are a joy to behold. The Daily Work will serve you well, in ways you cannot imagine. The journey begins with a single step in the right direction. *You* choose the direction, and your inner guidance leads the way. Focus on your inner voice so you may continue down the path to satisfaction and happiness. Maintain your center and inner peace with breathing techniques. Beware of your triggers, be aware of your thoughts, and you will achieve greatness.

Integrity

Building a sense of integrity may not be easy. It takes determination and dedication to one's goals and aspirations to follow through, *no matter what*. When your word becomes your bond, people hold you to a higher standard as their respect for you increases. Success—by your own definition—will be in your sights, as you build yourself from the ground up and from the inside out.

Become that reliable person—the one who stands out from the crowd and always acts in accordance with the way they speak, never deviating from their most genuine expression of themselves. You will meet others of the same merit and with the same willingness to do what is right, by their own finely tuned moral compass, without self-sacrifice.

If you feel drawn to explore the limits of your own integrity, by all means, do so. Just be warned that the less integrity you display, the greater your chances are of harming someone else and their freedom of expression. As explained in the chapters before, this is not a pleasant path to follow and this world is leveled out by justice at one point or another. So, do with that what you will.

Self-Dedication

Self-dedication can be seen as an extension of integrity. A high level of self-dedication is required if one desires to express great integrity.

You may develop and strengthen self-dedication by turning down your personal temptations, as discussed earlier. After you develop new habits, follow through with your original intentions, and achieve some of your goals, your self-dedication will be unbreakable, and your self-worth, trust, and respect will increase. This also builds self-esteem—something lacking in the world today! You must become a mountain of pure quartz—solid, stable, and only penetrable by the energy, words, emotions, and people you allow to impact you.

It is a tragedy to think of the great many people who give up on themselves for no real reason other than self-protection. Those who attempt to work toward their goals and dreams are often discouraged by others who do not see how these dreams can be achieved. So instead, mediocrity is chosen. This is part of the reason many people, after spending all day at a day job they hate, become energetically drained. They go home to eat something from the freezer, plop themselves in front of a TV, and continue like that for weeks on end—and we wonder why depression runs rampant! That is the real pandemic that nobody wants to talk about. Those who are in this very situation just ignore it like it's normal. Little do they know that all the power in the world lies in their own hands, waiting for their grand discovery! It is with this tragic reality that we suggest *you do not watch TV* more than occasional entertainment. Watching TV every day does to your brain what a microwave does to your food: it kills it.

Contemplations

- What is one of your most tempting temptations?
- What can you do to break the desirable ties with it? You don't have to hold yourself back forcefully (perhaps a bit of holding back is good for you), but it is much easier to become *unattracted* to whatever it is over time. How can you do that? Set the intention that you'd like to be shown a better way.
- Can you identify your most obvious emotional triggers? Where do they originate—childhood? An unhealthy relationship? Once you recognize them, ideally you will begin noticing them each time they trigger—then the real work may begin, ie. you may choose to step out of the hamster wheel of your old emotional pattern and purposefully choose a new path in that most intense trigger moment.
- What is one thing you would like to be more self-disciplined about—diet, exercise, the time you wake

up in the morning? Pick one to start with and set one challenging but achievable goal. If you leave your desires too vague, they may never manifest. We also suggest **not** to use the word "discipline", for it might create a battle with your inner child - the one who wants to rebel. So instead, it might be more motivating to focus on your "self-dedication" to achieve these goals.

11

Money

We are not financial advisors. You are responsible for your financial decisions.

The subject of money is often over-complicated and overly focused upon. Money, or the lack of (i.e. debt) is not designed to be the focus of life. It is quite simply a tool used to transfer energy from one form to another. If you lack money, you are cutting off your flow of creative Source energy. To remedy this requires you to go within daily, reestablish a connection with your True Self *every day,* and determine how you want to conduct yourself on this planet. Once you complete this critical step, you may move on to express the greatness bottled up inside of you, waiting to be released - your true passion. Then money will flow to you abundantly and it will cease to be your main focus.

Money is an important part of society. This is not evil, or wrong, or right (and let us just say here, if you don't love your money, someone else surely will). Money represents your energy. So, why has it become so easy to trust strangers to take your hard-earned money and make the best of it, with diversified investments you know little to nothing about? To save you time? Time to do what? What else is time good for besides creating great things you can be proud of with your precious collections of energy?

Sending your money off to some unknown entity who will use it themselves to retire handsomely is nowhere near your best interest, and in most cases, it would be better off invested in a place where you can see it and tend to it yourself. It might also be useful to contemplate the concept of diversification, for this could be considered a disbursement of your focusing power, which reduces its overall power (and is only good for those who do not have much self-trust to care for their precious energy expenditure). If you focus intently on one thing you are most passionate about, you cannot fail, and there will be abundance in one form or another.

Monetary Corruption

Many things may be said about businesses designed to take away the self-trust and self-responsibility of people who work hard all their lives, only to find it was all pissed away by a suit and a tie with a nice smile and a little lie. Elite financial institutions are talked up, like gods and royalty, setting up 401(k)s, mutual funds, and other types of digital securities, to make you think you can sit back and watch your money grow without your precious attention. While this may appear to work sometimes for some people, surprise, it was all a joke, a mere charade to take your physical gold! Now most assets are in digital form, as opposed to being held in some sort of physical form, which leaves them vulnerable to a failure of the electrical grid system... which would leave you with nothing—not even that little number on a digital screen. Doesn't this seem a little reckless?

Is it a trick, a trap? It happens across the global map—the debasement of money and the corruption of every single banking system. This monetary artistry has occurred throughout history, but children are given little to no useful financial education or even a hint of what caused the debasement. If children never learn about the historic, catastrophic mistakes that have brought down the greatest empires on the planet, what shall become of their future?

"No more gold," bankers and financial experts say. "It's a relic of the past. Let's digitize everything you have instead, so we can take it all in one simple grab! We'll digitize the equity in your house, all your retirement accounts, everything you've saved for your kids and your grandchildren." And then when you think they're done, they'll go straight for the kill shot: your health and good heart.

We've said it before and we'll say it again: never underestimate the power of self-sufficiency and self-protection, for that will hold you to the end. It was a bitter end for the Romans, once their government weakened their sturdy foundation with currency debasement (removing all precious metals from the coinage little by little over the years, causing inflation, debt, and poverty). This left them vulnerable to a collapse. Many other empires before them suffered the same fate. Just wait. The fall of the US dollar, which is now spread across the entire globe, will take the cake.

We suggest, with broken hearts, that you cut ties in any way you can with the mainstream digital financial system. It has the power to take everything you've worked so hard for. Time is ticking, but let this be a lesson to those who choose to hand off their self-responsibility to cunning, mischievous Beings, whom you think would have learned their lessons the hard way by now. The hard way is pending... Get ready. This one could be a bumpy ride. Buckle up, buttercup.

On a Brighter Note

While the above scenario seems pretty bitter and hopeless, let us remember what we have learned so far in these pages. Perspective and focus are where you hold the most power, and they allow you to create your destiny. You can change it today if need be. You are smart enough to educate yourself about money, on simple investments, and running a fun passion project or side business with your family. You don't need to hand everything to a stranger and trust their promises.

Let us now converse on the very bare-bones basics of money, so you may gain a broader and simpler view of your own financial situation and make decisions you can feel good about.

Tool for Exchange

Money is a tool used to exchange energy in a simple, measurable fashion. Some forms maintain their energy value over lifetimes. Some forms lose value as they sit. Yet, other forms increase. Each form has its time and place. It's your duty to yourself to learn of these forms and use their functions for your most beneficial outcome. For once you place your trust in another to do this for you, you are no longer assured that your energy is being used to *your* greatest advantage. Just as with health, financial responsibility is too often passed off to someone else, a "professional," if you will. While this may seem to work for some people, it increases your risk factor of loss exponentially.

Money That Maintains Value

The greatest money protectors of all time have been (and will most likely remain) precious metals like gold and silver and other commodity metals. Gold and silver have protected hard-earned wealth for generations. You will not likely enjoy bounty and riches with any get-rich-quick schemes. Hard-earned and hard-kept in your own hands is the best method and will remain such, no matter what noise and distractions others throw at you. If you are looking to *protect* some of what you have from loss and inflation, and third-party interference, this slow and steady method is the literal golden ticket.

Money That Loses Value

The next major type of money is the type that *loses* value over time. The longer you hold it, the less it will purchase, such as paper or fiat currency. This form of money is not really money at all, but rather it is a debt instrument issued by the Federal Reserve (which itself is neither federal nor a reserve). The paper represents debt, not real assets, since it is not created based on existing assets such as gold reserves. This paper is printed on printing presses and digital screens, with only the promise of our labor and that we will continue working for it, forever... Is this a form of... slavery? And who's we? The citizens of the world? Who created this deal again? The Federal Reserve and its unknown owners and the ones who think they can create layers above everything and say that they "own" it...

As the money supply increases over time, disproportionately to the growth of a country and its economy, inflation occurs. Spikes in prices of goods and services happen faster than wage increases, and the purchasing power of the new dollars decreases as it shifts hands, from the Fed, to the banks, to you. Thus, each time the Fed prints more, value is siphoned off the top, and the printing has to occur at an exponential rate the further into debt we go. Who benefits from this system? The people at the top who created it, because they have access to each new dollar first.

Let us remember, we're not here to point fingers or to blame unknown people. This has become a very complicated system. We are just here to say that once you see another way, you don't *need* to take part in this game full-time. Hard assets in your hands or under your management are a safe way to ensure your hard work pays off for you without losing value over time.[4]

---

[4] To learn more about the history behind this system, we recommend reading *The Creature from Jekyll Island* by G. Edward Griffin, and watching the YouTube channels "ITM Trading": https://www.youtube.com/c/itmtrading & "Gold Silver": https://www.youtube.com/@Goldsilver.

Additional Resources
    -All shamanism work and research by Michael Harner - shamanism.org
    -*Spiritwalker* by Hank Wesselman
    -*Fantastic Fungi.* Documentary. (Netflix)

Brief History of Fiat Currency

At its initial creation, fiat currency begins with hard backing, like gold and silver. That is the first step in bonding your trust to this paper (when the norm of society is to exchange solid gold or silver coins in everyday transactions, which are pure elements of nature and have no additional layers or contracts tied to them).

Once paper has been adopted (and remember, this is a multi-generational plan), the people in charge begin the excess printing, for themselves at first, and then their friends develop the great institutions to store and loan more paper to those who don't know what is going on behind the scenes - is there ever a lawful full disclosure? This debt slavery system plays well on human nature, which is an "I want it right now" mentality.

After a while, the metal backing can't be held up, for there is simply too much paper to compare to what's in the vaults. So it is best to cut ties with those pesky old relics of the past. They're too heavy, and who needs them anyway? We're on to a new age where everything is lightweight! Cue 1971 when President Nixon cut ties with the gold standard and effectively enslaved the human race via the exponential debt party.

Thereafter, inflation increases, and the loaf of bread that used to cost a quarter is now six dollars. But isn't that just normal? The economy couldn't look any better! A loaf of bread will always be worth the same, unless of course you're starving, or someone wants you to work harder to pay for everything.

Fast forward to "post-pandemic" and a mysterious virus caused supply chain chaos... But was that a charade, a fear blanket, to keep everyone distracted by yet another *thing*? Was all of that pandemic talk just a distraction and another way to point fingers so that this precious debt system is never identified as the greatest Ponzi scheme the world has ever experienced, and on such a grand scale, no one could ever believe it? All joking aside, the real pandemic is in your own untrained mind.

Money That Gains Value

The last form of money is the kind that can gain value over time. Many of these forms are illiquid, such as land, real estate, and collectible items, those you could not take advantage of their increased value unless you sold them. Keep in mind the proper perspective on this one also – scarcity drives value, but the currency it's being measured against is also losing its perceived value over time.

You may also enjoy increased value in a cash-flow entity you create, such as rental properties, or your own business.

Another perhaps more enticing or lazy method to increase your wealth is to put your money in a bank account and earn an interest rate—what an apt name! Something to catch the attention of those who are interested in more money without putting forth additional effort. Interest rates should only interest you if you are the one setting them for someone like you. Start taking an interest in your community and give fair loans to someone looking to start a small business with their family. This makes a country great, not putting every asset you have in a digitized form to be swept away into another realm beyond your comprehension.

Knit up the holes that have been singed in your small town, and make sure you have good ties with your neighbors and community members when things come tumbling down. For they will. It is only a matter of time. That is how this financial system was designed: to convince you to give most of your money away to someone else more educated or "worthy," who then takes the rest a little at a time either in interest payments (via your mort-gage ie. death-pledge) or inflation—taking pennies from your dollar every day, throughout the lives of your parents and grandparents, with no one ever noticing.

* * *

Fiat currency is a joke that has been played on humanity for hundreds of years. When you forget your past, and are never taught history in the way it happened, the same travesties will be repeated again and again. With our lack of a good form of financial education in elementary schools, society maintains the misperception that financial literacy is a looming challenge. We hope you take our words of caution to heart, for many great civilizations have been brought down because of the mismanagement of money.

Simply put, a country is left vulnerable for a hostile takeover, when its citizens have been so well prepared...

- With bellies (and blood) full of chemicals;
- With couch bodies on full display;
- With no ambition or life force to be seen or heard;
- With no gold in hand, or even mention of that word;
- With all financial value stored in a place far away;
- So the ones who take over can calmly stay,
- In their homes, all quiet and content,
- When they decide to pull the plug on the electric grid.
- And watch the chaos ensue, as the rats have nothing left,

- As was all part of this neat little plan,
- To digitize every... single... asset.

Back when you all had goals to strive for (goals other than paying off your debt), they had to go door-to-door to take your gold (1933 US Executive Order 6102). Now, all that good sense about saving money before making a purchase, or buying things you can actually afford, has faded. Schools are a joke regarding their lessons about history and financial literacy. Will they ever teach things that are so critically important? Perhaps that was all part of this grand design. To be as neat as neat can be. Remove beneficial education, incentivize families to split, confuse young people about how to identify, pacify them with TV shows and electronics. Enter their minds and take over (enter-tain-ment). Then, the makers of this strange matrix system can take everything from all people within an entire country, without their even noticing.

Express Freely Without Money

Do not deprive the world of your unique expressions because of your impression that you need money *before* you may do so. You don't—money comes after. Money comes as a byproduct of your exquisite inner happiness. As a Divine Creator, you are free to be as you please, and money will never hinder you in any meaningful way. It will flow, as that is how abundance is designed—to be everlasting, and free-flowing, for your simple pleasure and joy. Again, money is a tool. Don't focus on the tool. Focus on you.

Contemplations

- Do you often find yourself focused on money, or the lack thereof?
- Can you catch yourself in these moments and redirect your focus to a goal that is meaningful to you?
- What do you want to do when you have a lot of money? Create the feeling of unlimited resources as often as possible. You attract what you think!
- Do you have an idea for a side business you love to think about but you haven't made the moves to start? Decide on a small move you can make toward this goal, today and *every* day.
- Do you own any hard assets? What might be a fun and secure way to bring some of these into your investment portfolio (into your own hands)—physical metals, real estate, rental properties?
- Parents: What is one thing you can do with your children to teach them about money management or starting a business? Following their passion? Leading by example is always the best form of education.

12

Time

Time is important to discuss, because we spend so much precious energy worrying about it, or our perceived lack of it. It is valuable to remember, in your times of stress, that there is never too much or too little time. But if you feel you don't have enough, this is a signal that you're not focusing enough on the things you would like to be focusing on—a helpful signal to redirect yourself!

That we focus upon time at all is strange. Time is the equivalent of a tool, or a canvas, if you will, for you to use to express yourself. So, with this perspective, it wouldn't make sense to focus on or worry about a tool or a canvas, right?

Perceived Lack

The stress people put upon themselves in response to their perceived lack of time can create a ripple effect within their day-to-day life. Stress causes one to close their system up, resisting the world around them, which in fact generates more perceived lack —the more closed off you are to love, for example, the more lack you will experience. The more determined someone is to "have no time", the more this becomes a self-fulfilling prophecy whereby everything such a person touches becomes inefficient, stressful, closed up, lacking in everything they truly desire beneath their resentments.

The problem here is that such a person becomes identified with the story their ego has weaved, which is the story of lack— lack of time, or love or money— and how much of a *problem* this creates for their out-of-control reality. If you find yourself in such a space of lack or contraction, your focus is set on autopilot to search for this lack automatically. To refocus the eyes and see clearly once again, all it takes is a little balance, a couple deep breaths, and relaxation. Then you'll be able to reconnect with your heart and focus on where you time would be better spent to make you genuinely feel happy and content.

It is a great art and skill to create balance in daily life. It helps you maintain a healthy perspective so that you can conduct yourself immaculately. Without balance, you have chaos and misery (and most likely, catastrophe!) Keeping a steady eye on the present moment while maintaining focus on your heart's desired purpose is a balancing act, but a worthy one at that. Once one finds a good balance in life, time is no longer an issue to fight about, stress about, or ever again have any fear of "missing out."

To gain clarity and inner stability, and to make the best decisions, you must go about your days in a relaxed state. This skill will be necessary in times of unrest.

The Definition of Time

What is time? Is it a measurement? Is it the flow of another dimension? Perhaps it is a mechanism that helps us focus upon each detail of our creation separately, to experience the concept of separateness more deliberately. Perhaps time is a mechanism by which energy flows and is expressed, allowing it to condense into physical form more pragmatically than it might otherwise manifest.

Life does not flow linearly as your mind might expect. Life is fluid, like the ocean. This is the true nature of time and space: they are like a roller coaster taking us on a ride through this life that is one large entity *being*.

Is time real? We might say that it creates a level of resistance within the continuum, for better or worse. It is an illusion otherwise, a mere construct of your mind. Stop focusing on time to relieve unwanted resistance and excessive stress, and you will open one of the gates to achieving greatness—instant manifestation. It is much easier and more enjoyable to create without thinking about the background noise of time ticking away.

Time may be used as a method for transformation, for it provides the space *within* space to process emotions and trauma, release past baggage, learn who you are at deeper levels, and then manifest your dreams and desires into the physical realm. In other words, you can have a blank canvas in front of you on the physical plane, but without the "space" of time to create your artwork upon it, it would remain blank.

If the canvas of your life does not look quite right at the present time, remember, you do not need to forcefully or sporadically change your life, or blame your situation on people or events, or play the victim card when you feel you have no control over why your life appears as it does. When you see something you do not want, you must change your *focus* to what you **do** want, and then move incrementally in your preferred new direction.

You are not a rat in a race. You do not have to rush. As you become more focused and aware of how you're spending each moment, you will notice when you waste time, and you will stop doing things you discover are unnecessary. Time is a tool at your disposal to use as *you* see fit, so you can expand and bring great creations into the physical world. This most honorable purpose must be treated as such, for it is a significant part of this grand experiment we call life. It is an honor to be a part of this world, so let your light shine bright.

Time is a strange phenomenon. One minute you're here, another minute you're there, when really, *you* haven't gone anywhere - you are always *right here* on the cutting edge of creation. Perhaps space is also an illusion. Perhaps when we become the *observer* of space, it is akin to looking through a microscope. We must learn to continuously refine our vantage point so we may see clearly any situation we choose to face.

Time *outlines* our experience here. It creates a path that we as Creators may follow, to express Source into form, and to see how things are perfect or "good," as some spiritual texts say they are.

Live in the moment. What you want will appear at the proper time, as it is intended for a beneficial unfolding, for you and others in your life. It is unwise to concern yourself over things you lack, for concern only creates more of the same, hindering happiness and contentment.

Fear not the Unknown. It will always exist, so it is better and more powerful to develop comfort with it, and enjoy your time discovering what lies ahead. Remember, whatever challenges appear will always strengthen you if you allow them to.

Time is a tool. Use it wisely. Use it well.

Time Is Always Ready

What time is it? That is a charged question. Everyone stops to hear the answer, as if something magical is bound to happen. As we said before, time is a tool to express the infinite energy we have at our fingertips. Time is ready for our eloquent expression, at every second, every hour of every day. What are you waiting for? The best thing you can do is experiment. What is there to lose? A little money? A little sweat? For all you know, one of those experiments could become a masterpiece. How could you deprive the world of a grand original of your own?

Time Is Not an Obstacle

Time is not an obstacle. It is a tool for development, for creation itself. With its apparent linear construct, it is like railroad tracks leading off into the distance. You may walk along them, or you may step off. Remaining in the present moment will cause time to slow and even stop from your perspective. Practice makes perfect, which is why the Daily Work is so important. Maintain dedication to expanding your awareness of time, and you will begin to understand this secret-weapon mechanism so you can use it to your advantage.

Time Is Like an Obstacle Course

Time is like an obstacle course. You can only see what's right in front of you, unless you learn to broaden your perspective to more clearly see what's really going on, in your life and humanity at large. If you remain focused on your Soul Mission and remember your limited perspective, you will more easily trust The Way and be open to how life will deliver what you most desire. Questioning The Way with a lack of trust and hesitation will only create resistance and more obstacles on the path to achieving your wildest dreams.

Time Is Like an Ice Cube

Time is like an ice cube in a glass of water. It eventually melts and merges with its environment, completely unnoticed. Did the ice cube affect the environment? Maybe slightly—gave it a little chill, or a little wrinkle, if you will. Then it disappeared without a trace, like it never really existed in the first place...

Time Is Like a Treasure Chest

Time is like a treasure chest. Over your lifetime, you may fill yours with whatever you desire, and take out the things that you discover do not serve your highest power. The mistake many people make is leaving old, stagnant items to rot in their everyday thoughts, because they think they must hang onto these things such as self-hatred, fear, shame, and self-doubt. But alas, time is a storage facility you may use as you wish, and repeating the past in your head only holds you away from your truest source of bliss.

Identify and systematically remove things from your life you've outgrown or dislike. Only hang on to the memories and life lessons that bring you closer to alignment. The lessons that ring true will settle themselves into your heart as a permanent blossoming of your soul, so you may "level up" to greater challenges as you go.

By thinking of yourself as royalty and your time as a treasure chest, perhaps you will become more selective about what you allow inside your castle to begin with. If you think of time as a *treasure* chest, you'll be more apt to save only your most precious lessons and thoughts about yourself, those which you may be proud of forever.

Time Is Like a Piece of Paper

Think about time as a piece of paper. Each piece is a day in your time-space reality and so you only have one piece of paper in front of you at a time. Why would you be concerned about your future pieces of paper, day after day, when you haven't used the one right in front of you?

For the sake of environmentalism, don't waste the paper (time) you have now worrying about what might be in the future or what has happened in the past. The future always changes based on what you're doing and thinking *right now*. Remember this: Enjoy the moment. The rest is a blur.

Time Is Like an Icebox

Time is like an icebox always filling up with food, and the food being removed later. The box never changes, but its contents are replaced repeatedly. You see? Your depth of perception is what matters here. The box is existence, which itself is perfect and remains the same. The food represents your chosen expression on the physical plane, which is always changing and requires time for these changes to occur. But, holding onto some of these expressions or stories for too long will create a mess of rotten piles of rubbish inside your soul.

Do not fear what lies in the darkest corners of your soul (or icebox, or timeline), for they must be cleaned out, to ensure a clean slate (or the most optimal storage space for fresh creations). There is no need to hang on to old, rotten regrets of your past, or thoughts that hold you back from living in the present moment, particularly those based in a scarcity or a self-limiting mindset.

It is your right to do your "housekeeping" at your leisure (whether that be in this lifetime or the next). The sooner the better, though, if you are interested in making meaningful progress in your soul expansion now. Vibrational essences, Reiki, meditation (of course the Daily Work), and other energy healing practices are valuable if you are not yet ready to do your housekeeping alone. But ultimately, you are the only one who may clean out those corners. Honor thyself with these practices and you will indeed affect the world around you in beautiful ways.

> *Choose the path that makes you happy and fulfills you to your core. Dream big to go far and don't be afraid of a new door.*

Time Is Like a Popsicle

Time is like a Popsicle: drip, drip, drip, lick, lick, lick, and then it's gone. But you were not *inside* the Popsicle, were you? Did you disappear with it? No, no… but you did enjoy it! Or did you forget to do that, because it was melting and you rushed to eat it, so it wouldn't be "wasted"?

Time is meant to be enjoyed—the joy is in the journey after all. When you feel under pressure, time may feel like it's melting away, but you do not need to rush around, worrying about life dripping through your fingers like a melting Popsicle, for that just makes more of it slip away with no deeper meaning.

Remember, you are not *inside* the timeline, but rather you are the Creator observing and manifesting your creative endeavors within time and space. You are creating a physical manifestation of You. It's challenging to maintain this perspective when you allow yourself to become emotionally attached to ugly situations in your life. Remember not to cling to your beloved creations, or even worse, the situations which further ingrain your victim mindset! Focus on your passion, and if you don't know what that is, focus on figuring it out. As you learn to *notice* how you are using every moment of every day, you will start using more of your time to your advantage, and you will live out your days in a more pleasurable, relaxed state.

Time Is Like a Cavern

Time is like a cavern, a void within a solid mountain of rock. The void provides shelter, moisture, minerals, and darkness, and beautiful crystalline art forms are created, which cannot be created outside that environment. Time is such an environment for your own habitation and masterpiece creation—expressions that could not be manifested in such a way other than within this particular time-space. Your life, with all of its trials and tribulations, is your cavern. Your greatest creations might indeed already be formed as perfect crystalline treasures in the spaces of your soul you haven't yet dared to travel in. Travel to these places your fears block you from exploring, and you might be pleasantly surprised to find the keys for which you've been searching.

Time Is Like a Canvas

Time is an endless canvas at your disposal for eternity, if you like. You have freedom to do with it as you wish. If you are not enjoying your day-to-day life, what does your portrait look like? Paint your energy into something beautiful. Paint the most amazing thing you've ever seen. It is your job to figure out what that looks like.

If you are a great painter of energy, would you plan your future canvases before touching the infinite potential of the one right in front of you? Or would you take it, cherish it, and treat it as you would treat your child? Each stroke of your brush is perfection that will never come to fruition if you do not create it in the *present moment*. If you instead live in the past and worry about the future, you may never see your precious creations clearly enough to appreciate your accomplishments or feel the deep satisfaction you deserve.

Time May Bind You or Set You Free

Time may be perceived as a tool or a set of chains. Time does not restrain you—that is an illusion caused by a lack of focus on what matters in this life: getting to know yourself, and expressing your uniqueness wholeheartedly. It is not more complex than this.

If you feel bound by time, you are the keeper of your chains, and the key is within you, ready for your discovery! Focus on what you really want, and you will never again "lack time". If some things are not as you would choose them to be, be sure you are taking steps every day to change these. Small daily changes will add up quickly and will remove the illusion of chains you've created.

Once again, time is a way of communicating a masterpiece, bit by bit, so that the Creator may experience each part fully. This timeline experience is all for your unique, divine pleasure—so you can enjoy Creation in its fullest HD quality.

Time Is Not Money

Some people say that time is money. Time is not money. Money is a tool used to *represent* energy or to *transfer* energy from one form to another. Time is a tool used to *express* energy into physical form. These tools are not meant to be focused on, for why would you focus on tools? The creation at hand is what matters. Focus on what you're *doing* with the tools. Focus on learning who you are, what you like, and what you want to create. Then, money will flow abundantly (as it was designed to do), and time will cease to be a problem.

When you feel the time crunch, just relax, go with the flow, and everything will be okay. Tools are important, not evil, but they are not the masterpiece nor the grand finale. They only help you get there, as good tools do!

The Ultimate Rat Race

Life is not a rat race unless you choose to be a rat! Are you a rat, or are you royalty? You are in the flow of the time-space continuum, and believe it or not, you have chosen this reality for your expression. Do not take it for granted, yet do not get caught in a chaotic frenzy, either, unsure of which direction to turn, as time ticks away in your ear. Honor time as you are learning to honor and respect yourself.

Time serves as a placeholder for each expression you lay out on this physical plane for you to enjoy at your leisure. Universal abundance is at your fingertips, waiting for you to make your next move on this grand adventure! What will you create next?

To take full advantage of what you have in front of you, you must treat every moment as significant. Time should not be wasted on things you consider unimportant. Do not let time slip through your fingers like sand, for you are missing the point: to create greatness *within* and celebrate your accomplishments *without*. Have no fear, and nothing, not even death, can stand in your way to enlightenment.

Stopping Time

Time is an energy wave going from Source to Source. Once it reaches its destination, it piles up like an accordion. When you relax, time slows down and spreads out. When you tense up, time condenses and speeds up.

Measuring time linearly does not necessarily make sense on all levels of existence, because this speed-up/slow-down process happens locally. It is different everywhere (for each Creator). While certain community and global events may cause large-scale timeline alignments to occur between large groups of people, these alignments are only temporary, because so many other things are happening in people's lives that they are focusing on more intently. At any rate, theoretically, it would be possible to stop time for yourself by relaxing and going with the flow, releasing all resistance....

Contemplations

- Do you often feel rushed?
- In what situations do you say, "I don't have enough time"? Is this because you really don't want to do those things?
- What is it that you don't ever seem to have enough time for, that you really want to have time for? How can you make more time for it?
- Parents: What is one way you can teach your children to focus more intently on what they're doing throughout each day? It becomes easier to focus if they understand the benefit of each task for their growth and understanding of Life. Help them understand.

13

The Matrix

What is the matrix?

The matrix is a web of energy created by everyone involved with this planet. It could be compared to a garden—some parts are well-kept, while other areas are prone to neglect. This applies both to the physical world and your mind's own beliefs and patterns.

Part of this matrix is in fact known as the Garden of Eden—Heaven—Home, which is quite simply a very clear frequency found around the base of your heart, accessed by The Way through your ego creation. To come and go from this place at will is to be considered enlightened. The other parts of this matrix could be categorized into Purgatory i.e. mediocrity, and then perhaps Hell i.e. pain and suffering. Perhaps what you are experiencing now is based on how far away from your center you are.

There are many layers of this matrix we discover and intimately experience as our understanding of reality deepens throughout our lives. In a manner similar to the way moles dig their way out of the dirt and finally see the light at the surface, as human beings, we discover into adulthood that we've been living in the dirt until we learn to ground completely into our body, open our inner eyes, see the untended jungle of our mind, and begin doing the inner work, creating our Path through to Source, or Home, or what some might call the frequency of Christ.

What is your reality composed of? Muddy gray catastrophe, disasters everywhere you turn, or worse yet: mediocrity? If this is the reality you know, know this: *there is more*. If your life is depressing and devoid of life, you have focused your sight too much on the outside. This physical reality is quite elegantly the expression of your inner world, so if you want something else or something more, you must look within to remember your potential and who you really are. Do not be caught as a lifetime surface dweller.

The reality you live in is being drawn by your thoughts, emotions, and by the beliefs in your brain. Your deepest desires, when you get back in touch with them, will help you create what you want to see, originating from your heart to then be conceptualized by your brain. But, you must have a conscious, clear connection between your heart and brain for the manifestation process to function optimally. Manifestations that come directly from your brain might be driven by your undesirable thought patterns, cause problems in your daily reality, causing you to see things you may not desire to see. If you feel a lack of purpose, and do not know how to make your life enjoyable in a deep, fulfilling way, you may be operating too much in your brain.

Consider how many Creators, brains, and hearts there are on this planet. The more, the merrier really, like pixels on a TV. The more clearly each person sees themselves, the more clearly we, as a whole, can see reality. On the flip side, if everyone is trapped in their own dark, fearful confusion, self-hatred and abandonment issues, as a civilization, we become caught in our own undoing. This is part of the reason *you* are so important. Once you find the light, others will notice—you will brighten their lives, and the light will spread from there.

In a world where many people are depressed and have no ability to focus, it becomes easier to lie, cheat, and steal. There are more shadows to slink around in, but this cannot happen if everyone is conscious and clear within. That is the simple excellence of Creation and it is best left uncomplicated.

Complications Created by the Brain

The brain likes to complicate things that are best left alone, such as mistakes, regrets, the future, the past, politics, challenges in your relationships, temptations, bad habits, etc. These complexities are not your fault, but you must tame the beast inside your head so you can harness your divine nature and consciously manifest your desires into the physical world.

The whole point of this physical matrix reality is to understand yourself at deeper levels every way you turn. This structure is designed so you will never run out of novelty potential, and will always see room for innovation, thus feeding your desire to create and explore deeper levels of self-awareness.

Things here always appear to be changing, which is due to the continuous unfolding of your awareness, like a divine flower blossoming into eternity. The elemental structure and pattern of the matrix does not change. It is flawless, stable, and pure.

You must ignite the light within so you may spread it into

physical form. What does your light look like? If it is not unique, it isn't yours. If you desire to feel the great power and happiness in your soul, you must discover your unique factor and learn to express it into the world without hesitation or concern for what others think of you.

Conquering the Mind

We must now differentiate between two distinct frequency ranges that compete for your attention. Again, there is the portion that is most desirable yet continues to evade us, which is known as the Garden of Eden, Heaven, or Home. It is where all inspiration flows and things are manifested with ease, without a care in the world—pure peace—like Aladdin finding the magic lamp, successfully identifying and avoiding all the temptations and distractions before reaching that pure, natural state.

The other frequency range comes from technology and artificial radiation (cell towers, satellites, WiFi, radio waves, etc.). These things have made life easier and are great tools, but their usage has gone beyond the peak of their greatest benefit, to the point of causing catastrophic damage to societies around the planet, to our work ethic, to our motivation, and to our ability to connect with each other. These frequencies bombard our bodies, causing us to become ungrounded, distracted, and to forget who we are.

When you find yourself entangled by these artificially formed frequencies emitted by technology, you will also come to find that your untrained brain is detrimentally affected by the intruding energy waves, causing it to over-complicate things— your neural networks may look like untended weeds if you are not consciously tending to them.

Side Effects of Artificial Frequencies

The growing dominance of the digital universe is causing us to gradually focus more often outside of ourselves, leaving our internal world to rot. Setting the focus outside for too long causes us to lose sight of what really matters, creating an epidemic of both physical and mental health problems, and a total loss of personal power.

The digital world has become a trap for weak minds, but do know this is not a plea to call in the victim mindset. This is the next level of awareness we must step into so that our addiction to technology doesn't override our greater sense of purpose. As your perception shifts, you will recognize the signs and where you must form your own boundary lines between your personal energetic system and these artificial wavelengths, so you do not drown in the flood, so that you may break away at any time when you're in need of a recharge or something more deeply satisfying.

The artificial frequencies only stimulate you on the surface, and if you're not careful, they will drain your energy, using you up like a battery. They can only provide simple pleasures for your mind and body that may stimulate enjoyment for a short period, but after a while, you will feel the emptiness inside, which can lead to depression and may enhance self-destructive behaviors and addictive tendencies. If someone hops onto the downward spiral of unworthiness, self-hatred, etc., addictions may be pushed into overdrive including gambling, watching porn, excessive shopping, ingesting addictive substances, seeking out adrenaline and other physical pleasures. These are all energy drains that leave you feeling powerless and completely off your royal throne – your perfect centeredness, also known as Home.

Why are *you* here? What is your passion? What is your mission? Look within and discover this, or you will perish with those who never gave themselves a chance or never tried to find their real life source within.

Natural Frequencies

The natural frequencies emitted by Earth resonate with every cell in your body and can fully restore you to perfect health, if you allow this to occur. These frequencies enhance our capacity to give and receive love, and we do establish a footing in these health-restoring energies when we develop deep connections with others.

The Heart Grid is the electrical component of this, which is strengthened by physical contact (such as hugs). This is why social distancing and the digitizing of every single thing is undesirable, for the less we socialize in real life, in physical form, the weaker we become, physically, emotionally, mentally, and energetically as a whole. This Heart Grid thrives in small towns, where the community creates an energetic web of love with abundant friendships and the support everyone provides to each other. *This* makes the world a better place, and also provides some protection from the artificial frequencies and their side effects. If you choose to live most often in the digital world, be warned—for you will become this parasite's host.

The artificial frequencies can give you tunnel vision to the degree of being totally unable to see *what's on your mind*. Become a master of the Daily Work to observe how these internal energy waves—your thoughts and emotions—impact your external world.

Focus is Key

To be open enough to see your opportunities and to know where to focus, you must develop greater self-awareness. If you choose to be a serious player on this planet and stake your claim, your pristinely focused attention is key to the mastery of this mind-matrix game. That is why we say with great urgency: never let your mind run into the hands of another who does not care for your best interests. For example, when you find you have adopted beliefs that were established in childhood, or you discover beliefs you have picked up from other people or organizations over the years, catch yourself.

Beliefs close you off from seeing reality as it truly is. Catch yourself in the midst of arguments about politics and religion, as these are just other forms of enter-tain-ment to divide and conquer the masses, and to distract you from your life *within*. Catch yourself when you react emotionally to things you see on social media or TV. Catch yourself when you realize you're hanging on every word that comes from your most idealized celebrity, political or religious leader. You get the picture....

This artificial reality is a game where the big players of this world meet, to determine the fates of the savage and the weak. Choose not to gamble or fritter away your precious attention and time. You do not have to exist at that level—choose *not* to have a weak mind. Do you think great powerful people are boozing it up behind the scenes? Or is alcohol just another sneaky trap, set to catch those who don't yet see greater things to do or to be?

The world is interesting from the overhead view once you think critically about the things people do. You may wake up one day and realize the world submerged in these artificial frequencies is all just fluff—no substance, mostly lies. Wake up and realize that to conquer life, you must conquer your own mind.

> *This is where the big players play. Conquer your brain, or fade away.*

Heaven Can Be Yours Now

You may perceive your walls of limitation as a fish tank in the ocean, and what lies beyond is an infinite sea of abundance and life waiting to be explored. Call it what you will, but "Heaven" will suffice. It is yours for the taking whenever you decide.

There is no need to wait for death to experience Heaven, for waiting itself is akin to death. You are not using life to its potential if you spend all your time waiting for this, that, and the other thing to happen. Keep riding the wave and doing your best without resisting change. Relax and enjoy every moment of every day, *no matter what* is occurring in front of you. Yes, this is a challenge, but the better you become at relaxing, the easier it will become to appreciate *everything* that happens.

The reality you live in may not suit your current needs for expression, so do your magic and change what needs changing! There is nothing stopping you from having everything you've ever wanted. Go get it... or finish what you started.

Again, there is no need to sit quietly and wait. Don't waste your time slouching on the couch every day after work, zoning out and binge watching show after show. Do whatever feels right to you (and certainly relaxing is an important part of that), but keep in mind your intentions for every moment of your precious time. Know *why* you are using every moment as you are, with directed purpose from your heart. Only then will you feel free, whole, and content.

This divine flower is unfolding faster than we've ever thought possible, so it is helpful to remember that change is inevitable. How things will pan out is not known, but know this: *everything begins within.* It is within your power to take the reins and choose a better way of existing. Do it now - it's never too late!

Contemplations

- What is your unique factor? Can you describe it or identify it? If words are challenging, have you found ways to express it?
- What are you sharing with the world that, by your own standards, you consider great?
- Can you identify differences between the natural and artificial frequencies, and what the side effects look like in your life? (Hint: city vs. nature; brain chatter vs. free-flowing guidance from within; thoughts about past, present, future vs. lovingly creating your present moment with heart-centered passion.)
- What are some ways you could begin your detachment from these artificial frequencies and reground yourself into the natural energy of the Earth?
- What is something in your life you want to change, but have neglected? Why have you neglected it?

14

Pervading Stillness

Becoming still within... can you even fathom such a thing?

There are so many distractions to take you away from the one thing that matters: going within to meet yourself and accessing Truth, so you come to know and fulfill your purpose for being here. We are so preoccupied—so busy-busy, doing lots of little nothings to keep our minds *busy*. At the end of the day, these things do not fuel our fire for life, and many people feel lost, stressed, and empty inside.

Becoming still and genuinely at peace with yourself is a profound art form—something worth mastering if you desire to progress on the path to enlightenment. You cannot easily receive your inner wisdom if your thoughts, emotions, and actions remain chaotic.

Exercises for Becoming Still

Pause for a Few Minutes

To practice inner stillness, one must become a dedicated student of the work within, which starts with becoming present in your waking life. This, quite simply put, is the secret the greatest spiritual masters have taught throughout time.

If you give yourself a well-deserved pause in the busyness you're caught up in, your whole day will reset, and you will more easily develop your ability to focus on the present moment. Every day will be smoother; your interactions with others will be more enjoyable. You will develop access to deep Knowing, clarity, and purpose, so you make the best decisions (with less resistance).

The practice may begin simply, with five minutes of dedicated stillness a few times throughout your day. It doesn't matter where you are—take five minutes with eyes closed upon waking, five minutes as you make your coffee, five minutes before stepping out of your car, five minutes before you fall asleep. Focus on your breathing and see what comes up in your mind, or fantasize about achieving your most exciting goal, and the way to it will gradually become clear.

The more often you reflect or contemplate (even if it's just for those few minutes at a time), the more you will experience all your troubles fading into the distance. Breathe *deeply*. Exhale *fully*. The greatest minds in the world will attest to the *power in the breath*.

Accept and Let Go

Holding on to old thought patterns, resentments from childhood, and grudges only causes *you* harm—no one else. Sometimes we might hang on to these things, thinking we are expressing ourselves in a useful fashion, when in actuality there is something within these stuck patterns that requires processing and self-forgiveness.

It is possible to *let go* of any feelings you do not enjoy and thoughts that do not serve you quite effortlessly once you *accept things as they are*. As you learn to witness these injured parts of you, of your past, the closer you will be to inner stillness and enlightenment. Once you are no longer a *slave* to your brain, to your ego, to emotional reactions, or a guilty conscience, you may use your brain for its greatest good (which is, again, to capture and conceptualize inner wisdom, and manifest it into your waking reality).

Becoming still within—holding a crystal clear frequency within your body—allows the free-flowing stream of universal consciousness to flow through you effortlessly. Keep in mind that while you will witness miracles, things will not always be pretty. To be wise means exploring all avenues, accepting all parts of yourself and reality without fear and without turning away in disgust or with judgment. This is why the ability to let go, coupled with precise movement and gentleness toward yourself are so vital. The less pleasant parts of life will take time to explore and process but will provide depth to your character and a greater comprehension of reality and the manifestation process.

Follow Universal Law

Universal Law (having mercy, showing respect and honor, acting with dignity and courage, etc.) assists in your day-to-day tuning and inner stillness. Keeping these laws in the front of your mind is imperative when you are around highly emotional, "sloppy" or energetically fragmented environments. Chaotic surroundings provide opportunities for you to practice cutting through the noise and to remember that no person, tragedy, or circumstance can penetrate your energy field unless you *choose* to let it in. This level of inner stillness is a rare, invaluable commodity, and once you cultivate it, it will spread like wildfire amongst those who are receptive to it.

> *There is no denying pure Truth when it is spoken or heard. It penetrates deeply and its validity is unquestionable as it sinks into your core.*

As you achieve greater stillness, you will see the light you wish to see in this world. Use those around you as mirrors—as clues to your own inner cleansing.

Patience & Relaxation

As you become still, you will discover that you have plenty of time for all the things you really consider important, and you won't feel the need to rush around so much anymore. You will be more willing to give each moment of the day the care and attention it deserves, and so everything you do will be of greater quality.

Take time to take care of yourself. Exceptional self-care indicates a high level of self-respect which develops into greater comprehension of your true self-worth. Give yourself a break. Ample rest is important for your well-being and your continued progress in this work. If you do not get enough sleep, relaxation, and fun, you will burn out (and so will your patience). Some people feel they need permission to take a break. If you need to be that person, by all means! Don't forget to give yourself permission, too.

Are you putting yourself under pressure? Remember that you cannot rush the unfolding. Pressure creates resistance, which slows your progress and hinders your enjoyment of the moment. Every moment is significant, so a feeling of impatience may indicate some level of disconnect from reality—a desperate desire to control your surroundings, stemming from a wound within you—perhaps an insecurity? Try to find peace with *why* things are panning out as they are, especially if they are not happening the way you expected or within your expected frame of time. When the time is right, you will understand more fully, and you will discover that everything is flowing into place perfectly, even if from a much broader standpoint.

Patience is a virtue that we all struggle with to some extent. Trust The Way, for it will lead you to everything you've ever wanted, and more. Listen to your heart's needs by, quite literally, asking it what it needs…. and then following through.

To become patient and maintain a steady frequency requires your whole energy system, body and all, to be clear and at peace. The key? *Choosing* to relax and be still…

- Be still in moments of disagreement.

- Be still when a situation is flooded with uncertainty.
- Be still when things lose their sense or clarity.
- Be still when you find yourself searching frantically for answers which do not come.
- Be still when you have no words to give, and the best words will flow unhindered while you simply bear witness to the Truth unfolding around you.
- Be still, and you will speak in a manner unknown to your race, yet the words will be so penetrating, they will not be ignored. For the Truth shall always be heard, down to the core of every Soul.
- Be still and Know.

Relaxation is a major part of becoming still, but to achieve deep relaxation requires the identification and release of old tension patterns. If you do not know where to start, energy workers (such as those who practice sound healing and Reiki) can be valuable, as can practices such as Tai Chi. If you hold tension in certain areas, even after massages and chiropractic work, it might be time to go a little deeper. To heal physically, you must get to the root of the tension, which is deeper than the physical body.

Rooting out all tension is a vital part of self-care. Start considering relaxation as an art form that you can become proud of. If you are not taking time for yourself to unwind every day, this will cause damage to your body. Again, you can begin this practice easily, right now, with five minutes. You will see why Zen masters spend hours in meditation. It is their way of honoring themselves and maintaining their dedication as a student of The Way.

Once you have sparked your fire and achieved a deeper level

of stability in your relaxation practice, your inner clarity will increase substantially. Continue with the daily practice, for it allows you to touch the inner flow more consistently, bringing peace and enjoyment into every moment (you'll know it when you see it).

It is an honor to be expressing yourself in form as you are. Treat yourself with the respect you deserve. You may already know many of the things we speak of here, yet they are worth repeating, as they will forever be a practice, never perfected.

Contemplations

- Can you bring the five-minute breathing exercise into your daily routine?
- How many times in one day can you remember to do it?
- When you're stressed out about something, can you remember to do it in the worst moment?
- What is one way you can allow yourself a break in your hectic schedule, if you don't already do so? Can you set aside a full 30 minutes to just unwind and do whatever *you* want, without guilt-tripping or pressuring yourself?

15

Manifestation

Manifestation is the mechanism by which one expresses their desires into the physical world. It's about *action*. Figure out what you want to do, then go do it, even if it's a tiny step at a time. There is no need to do it all at once; the joy is in the *journey*, not the destination, after all. Once you break your goals down into *daily* steps, it becomes much easier for your brain to comprehend your success.

> *Use your brain, don't let it use you.*

Manifestation does not have to be challenging. You have manifested your current reality by your thoughts and emotions alone, which may be hard to believe (and perhaps it's preferable to deny this sometimes if you're not in the position you'd like to be in). Even the most unpleasant life circumstances are brought to you by what you believe about yourself and the reality around you. It all makes sense when you observe your inner world, thoughts, emotions, daydreams, deep unconscious patterns etc., and then compare them to what unfolds outside of you. Of course, there's a bit of a time delay between what you think and what comes to be in the physical—and such delays are often beneficial! So, what can you do if your life is not how you want it to be? Start by monitoring your thoughts and emotions.

Monitor Your Thoughts

People get into the habit of complaining about inconsequential things. If you catch yourself doing that, and replace your complaints with constructive, loving thoughts and emotions, that will change your world significantly. Behave as though *all* your thoughts, feelings, words, and actions are leading your life—because they are.

When you learn to take command over your *response-ability*, you can change your life. To start, become aware of the thought patterns that do not move you in the direction you want to go. These thoughts are often tied to the ego, and are not always desirable to let go of! Once you have identified the problematic thoughts (which is the hardest part), you can manually replace them with thoughts that do move you in your desired direction.

For example, if you often complain or think about not having enough money, or stress about your bills, or feel like a victim of life, instead tell yourself something like, "I'm excited to see how money comes to me easily and abundantly". Catch your thoughts when you have another bill to pay—instead of being angry, think about how grateful you are for what you do have now and your comfortable living standard, compared to many others. Repeating this gratitude practice enough times will slowly change your belief systems. To speed up this process, as noted in the next section, take time to *feel* what it would be like to have plenty of money all the time. Feel the gratitude you would have with such plentiful resources flowing into your life. This will more actively change your life.

Let us say you have a problematic relationship with someone, such as deep childhood resentment towards a family member. Think of this resentment as an overgrown, tangled weed living off your bond with this person. The weed is fed by your energy every time you feel that resentment flare up. So here we have identified a common energy leak most people are not aware of. Let this awareness serve as a motivating factor to begin trimming this weed, even if just simply to save your energy for more important things!

Certainly there is no pressure to do this weed trimming all at once. Years of neglect create deep roots and large tree trunks! Believe it or not, just putting your loving attention on this weed will start the healing process with this person. Your life will offer opportunities to mend the bond between you, and then it's your job to override your ego and take the opportunities when they appear.

Monitor Your Emotions

The next area to work on is emotional triggers, such as the resentment mentioned in the previous section. This can be challenging because emotions come with a host of chemicals the body becomes addicted to. But, as a Creator with bigger and better things to accomplish, you have the power to put the emotional roller coaster to rest—and anyway, most of these situations with other people are an energy-taking contest that only fills one person temporarily and leaves the other person drained. This is not a morally sound or productive activity. Manually taking control of yourself when you are triggered and reminding yourself, for example, how grateful you are to be where you are, is one of the easiest ways to redirect your emotions and stop this type of sorcery transaction from occurring.

Another critical component to conscious manifestation is to think about whatever it is you want, say, a load of money or a beautiful romance, and then *feel* what it would be like if you had it *right now*. If you find yourself thinking of your most exciting desires with a feeling of longing, jealousy, self-pity, or doubt, you are creating a vicious circle and you will continue creating exactly what you see now—reasons to be jealous, reasons to be left *wanting*. In that moment of recognizing this problem, manually replace those feelings with the good feelings you want. Again feel the gratitude for what you have and that you are worthy of so much more.

After working on this "replacement therapy" for a while, if you don't notice the changes in your life that you expect, don't give up. It takes time to build habits and momentum, like a train switching directions, building power and speed takes a couple minutes. Remember to pay attention to your inner world, and process what comes to the surface. Relax, breathe deeply, exhale fully—and enjoy the miracles. The path will always appear differently than you expect.

> *If you do not expect greatness, you will not receive it.*

Fate

Fate is quite misunderstood. When people hear that word, uneasiness comes into their eyes, arising partly from fear, and partly from uncertainty or a lack of understanding. Some people may think they are doomed to a lifetime of suffering because they feel guilty about things they have done in their past, or they simply feel that their fate was set to condemn them forever, from their conception. If you are worried about being sent to a "fiery place of damnation for eternity," someone has done a good job striking you down with some deep-seated fear.

The Fates were portrayed in Greek mythology as three women weaving the threads of fate of everyone and everything on this planet into the future. We suggest that these threads of fate are being woven *now* in the present moment. The present moment (which is always upon us) is the cutting edge of reality. Nothing beyond the present moment has been written. Certainly, some patterns may be predicted, but these predictions are based on *current* energetic patterns. Likely many of these patterns/threads are those you choose to maintain from your past, so it is within your power to drop those threads whenever you desire, and grab hold of the threads that will lead you to your most beautiful future.

Everything can change in the blink of an eye if that is what you *choose*. You have the power to change your world and the trajectory of your life right now.. If you decide to change your life *and act on it* now, your fate will shift closer to your vision of your perfect future. Of course, if you make a meaningful change today, and go back to your old ways tomorrow… well, you don't need a psychic to predict what will pan out.

The Way is the road less followed for a reason: it isn't always easy to stay on track. The good news is that the hardest part is taking those first steps, developing new habits, taking responsibility for your life, for your happiness, and taking action every day toward your goals, while making time to take care of yourself. Love your soul, and nothing will stand between you and the most beautiful fate you can imagine.

Remember, you hold your fate in your own hands. You have only today to choose your threads of fate, so make it count, make it your best, for tomorrow does not exist. If you don't, what will become of your life? To manifest anything you wish, maintain directed, confident focus on what you desire most. That is the greatest secret: you may have *anything* you want without forceful action or suffering. When in doubt, just relax. Do not be your own worst enemy, believing you do not deserve to attain your goals, dwelling on "what ifs" or trying to accomplish everything at once. Develop patience. Enjoy and appreciate the journey day-by-day, for that is where genuine joy exists to be felt.

* * *

Once you have achieved certainty somewhere in your life, that is your signal that you have made meaningful progress on your inner path. Just be sure this is in fact certainty, and not you closing yourself off to further progress. Being certain from your center, from your throne, from Home, allows you to maintain a level of openness, so that you may always be confidently flexible under any circumstance.

Instant Manifestation

Instant manifestation requires self-forgiveness, inner stillness, patience, harmony, and balance between all co-creative partners. As you develop your energetic foundation, you will see the energy at your fingertips come to life. You will begin to observe how *all* the things that come into your life are a result of what occurs within you *first*. It will astound you. Continue to follow Universal Law and develop the habits needed to reestablish your naturally clean frequency. You will uncover a *total* feeling of security and perfect clarity within yourself that will be undeniable.

> *Move through life gently, like a mother with her young, with firmness and clear intention so you can manifest perfectly using your carefully directed attention. Follow your intuition without hesitation.*

You may come to a point in your path where near-instant manifestation not only becomes possible, but is simply *logical*. This becomes easier as you continue on; there is no need to force it. Trusting yourself is critical—it will free you from the bindings your environment appears to place you in. In time, these will fade. You will see reality for what it is—and is not. Remember, you are not who you *think* you are. Peace and harmony will be your shining lights and will serve as guideposts in the darkness as you become a beacon for others.

Treat your life as you would a fine work of art: delicately, precisely, with purpose, and a great deal of appreciation and satisfaction as you gaze upon your progress.

When you are unhappy or unsatisfied, do not hesitate to make changes. It is critical to sit with yourself *every day* and contemplate your life. Where are you and where do you want to go? Are you moving in your desired direction? If not, you may need to release excessive resistance left over from your past. It's okay to have some level of resistance to maintain structure and healthy boundaries in your life. This is a balancing act.

Resist only to the degree necessary to affect change in the physical realm, and remain as fluid as water or formless energy when discovering the newness within.

Develop and achieve goals for your creations (a form of resistance, goals are a structure for your energy to flow), but do your best to remain open to the ever-present never-ending possibilities, which have the potential to change all of your plans in an instant. By achieving the inner precision and balance you need for your most optimal expression, you will lead the way to true happiness and contentment for yourself and others—and that is how the wildfire of Truth begins. Once people realize they have within them the greatest source of power on the planet, the confidence in their manifestation ability will overtake all other untruths. Truth cannot be stopped at that point, and your world will never be the same after that. You (and much of the world) will experience a significant transformation, one long overdue and imperative for your survival on this planet.

Steady as Stone

Learning how to manifest instantly can be an excellent achievement—or it can be disastrous. Think of the story about Jesus manifesting enough loaves of bread and fish to feed the masses. That was excellent! Now think of the last time you had a nasty thought about someone you love, perhaps a time you wished that something bad would happen to them. This is why, at this stage of your development, one thought is not that powerful, so you experience a time delay between thoughts and physical formation. Instant manifestation is possible, but only for those who have developed a *very* clear, steady mind and heart.

How to Achieve Instant Manifestation

- Do unto others as you would have them do unto you (and vice versa).
- Behave with kindness, respect, dignity, and have compassion for all.
- Listen to the small voice within until it becomes loud and clear.
- Say what you mean and mean what you say.
- Show courage, and step through your fears.
- Monitor the ego - your response-ability.
- Consciously express all words and emotions. Be precise in everything you do and say. Do not get caught up in an automatic reaction to an old replayed memory in your brain.

- Accept all parts of yourself—your most loved traits and things you're embarrassed of.
- Be the light in the darkness, and witness the world unfold around you perfectly.

Absolute certainty is key to manifestation. You must feel certain that what you want is coming to you bit by bit, every second of every day. Step through the foggy illusion of fears.

Your Body Is a Masterpiece

Is the denial of the physical world and the physical body causing us to lose manifesting power? Is this what caused us to leave the Garden originally? Some say the five senses are a lie, a mere illusion of this life. Some great religious leaders say the five senses are proof of a sinful existence... but what if to deny your five senses is to deny your greatest tools of manifestation? This denial or belief that this world is sin and that we are sin, is not a way to get in touch with our true source of power.

Let us say the body is a pen, for example, and the soul is the ink. Perhaps when we are fully aligned with the body—no longer hating parts of it, *fully* loving and honoring it as the very excellent home that we ourselves have created—this is like ink finally coming to the tip of the pen and writing fluidly without hesitation (instant manifestation). Then it's just you, your blank canvas of Earth, and time to create whatever your heart desires.

The physical body is the perfect vessel for receiving this heart-derived knowledge and manifesting it into the physical realm. There is not a more exquisite fashion for this great unfolding of the Universe. Your physical expression is how your soul desires to be expressed (unless you are suppressing yourself, which becomes obvious over time via wrinkles, health problems, and diseases... ugliness). The unique physical form which you bring to this world is the pure creation of your destiny, as it lies right now in this moment. Treat your body as the great creation it is, for it deserves to be honored and respected. It is the holder of divine royalty after all!

Developing Creativity

As Divine Creators, it is our duty to create unique works of art, in whatever form is right for you. Do not get caught in the trap of *thinking* you are not creative, since your very existence *is* creativity itself. To deny your innate creativity is to deny your true nature, which is detrimental to your happiness and will dampen the light of your soul.

To develop creative potential (if you feel you are lacking it), begin the Daily Work. The greatest creative treasures lie within you. They are just waiting for your discovery so you can manifest them into the physical world. Nothing outside of you can fill you with the satisfaction you need. Those outside of you can provide you with some, yes, but externally-provided fulfillment or validation does not penetrate your core in the same deep way.

Try going back to your youth, to a time before the light inside you was covered up. Reexamine what you, as a child, focused on instinctively. Those things will be your most potent points of creation. Once you relearn this natural exploration of the soul, you can create the most beneficial environment for your own children and grandchildren to create in and explore. Then, you may move beyond the current rat trap of existence into an infinitely more beautiful planet of co-creation!

> *Fear not the Unknown, for that is the most blissful path toward the enlightenment you seek.*

Contemplations

- Can you identify one common thought you have that is negative? Sit with it and see where it leads you, such as a childhood memory. Ask yourself what truth it has in this present moment.
- Do you believe you are worthy of creating what you'd define as greatness? If not, what would it take for you to believe you really can do anything you want to do?
- As you learn how to "dial" yourself in and fine-tune your frequency (including thoughts, emotions, what you say, how you act, and even your food and beverage choices), what is the first great thing you want to manifest?
- Do you consider yourself creative? Since this is a foundational part of who you are, what can you do to explore this part of you more, if you aren't already well versed in your own creative expression?

16

Inner Truth

Inner Truth is a beauty to behold. Once you are shown The Way, you can never unsee it. You will Know, and you will have to go. It will become your strongest desire, your only meaningful urge. Once you have one taste, you'll want to taste it every day. Like the eternal drug, it will leave you forever changed.

This book has presented introductory guidelines for how to access Truth so that you may more easily manifest anything you desire. Your external expression is a reflection of how clear your inner channel is — how much Source energy is able to flow through you and out into the world. Clearing this channel is the only game in town for those who desire true happiness and fulfillment (…and less wrinkles and body degradation).

In this final chapter, we will reiterate a few things and add a few more tools intended to help integrate your new clarity and guide you as you continue along your path of enlightenment.

Accessing Truth

The answers to all the questions anyone has ever asked are held within you. All you must do is ask, sit quietly, and listen. The answers will come, but it requires a little patience and self-dedication. Those who Know this have the world at their fingertips.

Spending too much time in the external world and ignoring this internal wisdom will cause one to feel empty and void of purpose. Seeking excessive attention and lavish lifestyles will not fill the void when material things lose their luster and all the shallow people leave. Ignorance of your True Self has the potential to manifest into health problems and other types of personal turmoil. Any evidence of a rotting soul means there is a lot of Work to be done. You can only ignore the Truth for so long.

Nothing can stop the Truth from being Known, for it originates deep within the cores of all natural-born. Your clear channel is the most valuable, sought-after treasure of them all. You may find clarity within once you learn to accept and forgive yourself. How? Know you already are the things you most desire: confident, courageous, healthy, attractive, etc. You are now unraveling the false identity you and the world have placed upon you, so you can return to your pristine, illuminated Self.

* * *

Remaining connected to Oneness is a practice, but is the way to most easily manifest your deepest desires. Do not get discouraged. It requires patience and diligence…

> *You must be prepared to say what you mean and mean what you say.*

No flying off the handle, even when you're alone (hello, anyone who's ever driven a car). Remain centered, relaxed, and confident. You are royalty, after all—act like it. Do not be self-righteous. Be a humble servant, lighting the torches of the world. Be pleasant, even in places and around people who do not fit your style. You must remember your humbleness so you are not a detriment to yourself. If you think you are better than others, that becomes an easy downward spiral to misery and catastrophe, as you identify with your ego and cling more and more to your external reality to feel worthy. You will not be happy, for happiness doesn't exist in those off-center ego-driven spaces.

To maintain perfect alignment is both a skill and an art. Go with the flow, but do so consciously. You will know when you're connected, and others will see it. You will spark the light in people's eyes, the deep recognition—it will be obvious when it happens.

It is essential to your harmonious day-to-day living that you achieve *consistent* awareness of the Oneness that connects us all. Keeping this at the front of your mind is key to maintaining your centeredness. If you can see yourself in everyone and everything, there is no logical reason to fight, act from your resentments, or curse at the driver who just cut you off (he might be shitting his pants, after all).

Think of yourself as a universe surrounded by many other universes, colliding in infinite ways. Disturbances will occur, and it is up to you to manage these. Shift your perspective; choose the most beneficial response regardless of your ego. Keep in mind, too, if another universe collides with yours in a destructive or disruptive manner, altering your frequency to match theirs could be detrimental to you. It is best not to "catch" someone else's discordant emotions (they are contagious). It can create an emotional pandemic, and you have the power to stop it from spreading! Maintaining alignment and a broad perspective, and remembering to appreciate everything around you will alter your experience, and you will be less likely to react unconsciously.

Home Is Within

Here in this matrix we call home, you might wonder, what is "home?" They say, "Home is where the heart is" and "…from the bottom of my heart…" What does this mean? Could this be taken literally?

Home is where you may celebrate your most cherished sense of Self, and express yourself freely. It is the sacred space where love is in abundant supply, free for your receiving at any given time. This place is within you, and can be found by connecting with your heart center—the base of your heart, as we mentioned before.

There are two cherished homes we might consider here: the one you see externally, that you share with those you love most. The other is internal, and is meant for you alone. Home is a cherished ideal for many people. When you go within for a few minutes every day, you give yourself a chance to regroup and discover how you feel about certain things in your life, so you may go about your daily business with a confident outlook and in a precise manner, with a clearer understanding of where you're headed. Quiet your mind and listen. This task is quite simple but at first may not be easy, but you will always be rewarded for your patience and perseverance.

Going home brings joy and happiness, offering you relaxation at its finest. If you haven't done the work within, it's hard work to rely on your external reality to bring you what you want. If you want your external home to be that beautiful place you've always wanted—a warm, loving environment to rest your head—come Home within yourself, and you will have everything you've ever wanted.

How to Come Home:

- Sit up straight, feet on the floor or stretched out in front of you – no crossing.
- Put your focus, your point of awareness, at the base of your heart.
- Take a minimum of five deep breaths in and exhale fully each time (get all the old air out).
- Notice the shift that occurs during these five breaths. See how quickly this shift can happen once you have more practice.

During these five breaths, you may notice anxious thoughts going through your mind. Continue breathing. They will pass. A bonus to this exercise is that you can do it anywhere. When you understand what this "centered" feeling feels like, you can carry this skill with you and go "there" every chance you're able to. This is the "home" you will become accustomed to. It will be your favorite place to go. See for yourself!

Self-Trust

Trusting yourself is critical to your expansion and fulfillment. Come to know your most important needs—and honor them. Do not let others pressure you into thinking that what you're doing is "wrong." Something is only "wrong" if it is vibrationally misaligned for *you*. They can't truly see what is right for you. Only you Know—and it's your duty to find out what it is, and trust yourself more than anyone else.

Under no circumstances *sacrifice* yourself (especially for someone else's benefit). Even the littlest things you agree to, begrudgingly for someone else, will break down your self-respect, which ripples out into others' opinions and feelings of you. You may help others, but only help those who desire to help themselves, and only do so to the degree which does not deplete you nor impedes progress toward your goals. If you overflow in resources and self-love, you may share the excess— that is what it's made for. If you do not overflow and then deplete yourself further (like most of the population) because of some guilty feeling that you must give back more than you have... who are you helping? You're actually causing harm to yourself and all of existence.

Learn to listen to your heart. You will perceive Truth naturally in the moment, as it was always meant to be perceived. Trust you will be fine, and that all will go perfectly, as it always has, and always shall.

Unravel Your Conditioning

Conditioning can be undone with proper inner guidance and the intention to become more aware throughout daily life. To begin the unraveling process, try taking these statements deeper into yourself with meditation:

- Life itself is a gift, and an achievement worthy of celebration.
- Cherish each moment as if it were your last, for each moment truly is.
- Behave in every instant as the royalty that you are, for this will come to change your everyday life before your eyes.
- Be brave, be bold.
- Be yourself, no matter the circumstances.
- Choose honor over indecency, no matter what.
- Choose your words wisely, for thoughts have a much larger energetic impact once spoken.
- Learn to clean up your thought habits, for they too have an energetic impact on all of existence, and why add to the clutter if it is unnecessary? Save your energy!
- Lastly, remember to monitor and rein in those out-of-control emotional roller coasters. Your health and your loved ones will thank you!

Limit Your Screen Time

To be in full alignment with Source energy, you must maintain conscious awareness of your center at all times. Never let yourself become absorbed in the brain too long. When you lose touch with the internal realm, you are more easily tangled in the chaos of your external experience. This can happen while you are using technology or staring mindlessly at one of your digital screens. If this inner path is the path you desire to continue on, stare at a fire instead, or at the back of your eyelids while you contemplate your next goal or creation.

It is a habit of society with so much technology to spend many hours doing basically *nothing* while time ticks on. Who has time to waste on violent shows or poorly produced cinematography, anyway? Yes there are a few exceptions, as some cinematic artistry is of a high caliber and deserves to be applauded for its mastery in storytelling. But let's leave it at that—the TV ought to be an *occasional* enjoyment to be shared with family and friends. The rest of your time must be spent unraveling your mind, so you may feast your eyes on your own grand designs!

Be Aware of Expectations

Do not bar yourself off from infinite potential by developing limiting, or rather ANY, expectations of others. Creating and *clinging to* expectations for others to align with increases your chances of disappointment and resentment. This is of utmost importance to remember in regard to your family, friends, romantic relationships, and especially "situationships"! You are free to set expectations for yourself, but do so without setting yourself up for failure. As well, when working with others, do your best not to set them up for failure, either. Do your best not to cling to your imagined outcomes of events in your life. Maintain your composure no matter what happens. These are your tickets to greatness! Do with them what you will.

> *You want the answers to life? Maybe you are the answer to life, as simple and perfect as that.*

Improve Intuition

There are only so many compositions you might create in a day. It is your job to choose those which serve your Higher Self. This is where developing an awareness of your intuition is useful—and critical. Practice listening to your gut instinct; it will serve you well. Your intuition is one of the most important tools you have access to, to get into "the flow," and to make day-to-day life easier, productive, and more enjoyable. It allows you to achieve your goals faster than you can imagine.

To develop an "ear" for your intuition, meditate daily. Follow (*& do not ignore*) your gut feelings. The more you listen, the more obvious they will become. This is easiest while driving, as you learn to anticipate the sudden decisions of other drivers so you can respond perfectly with perfect timing. You may also take notice if you have young children who act like young children do and run around, sometimes, without noticing where they are, or put weird things in their mouths! A mother's (and father's) intuition anticipates disasters, allowing you to avoid most of the worst accidents. If you enjoy cooking, you can develop a sense of intuition here, too. Parasite cleansing also helps.

Do your best and nothing less. The key to perceiving your intuition is to be calm at all times. Take a moment or a breath *before* allowing someone or something to trigger you. Just *be*.

Use your breath as a tool for staying focused. Can you imagine how miraculous and easy life would be? Perhaps you are seeing the endless possibilities!

Self-Worth

Focus on yourself. As you may discover, *you* are the most relevant and useful "thing" you can work on in this life. To focus on yourself daily will change your life in powerful ways. Dedicate time to clearing out your environmental noise and accumulated baggage. Start anew every day.

Most people are never taught to access their self-worth (hence the rat race). Most cannot even fathom the depths of satisfaction and confidence they may achieve by doing this inner work. It is possible to reveal self-worth in adulthood, but it requires one to be dedicated to one's Mission. If there are to be any worthy and capable leaders when future times demand such, you must take this work seriously. You will know when such times arrive—others will be waiting for you to teach them.

Nurture your soul, cherish who you are becoming, as well as who you have thus far become, for there is much to be said about such bold, precise progress. One major step in building self-worth requires you to figure out what it takes for you to respect *you*. To get there requires daily commitment and a *desire* to get to know yourself and what you want. There is no shortcut. What is it you want out of life? As we've said before, you do not need to define yourself by one thing alone. So, the better question is, what do you want out of this life *right now*?

Do not be embarrassed by the seemingly small or childish requests that first come to mind—those are your personal flair, and they keep the fun alive! They are *all* important and should be enjoyed. But once you get down to the nitty-gritty—once you get to your big, long-term goals—ask yourself if you are taking steps *every day* toward those goals. Daily action feeds your self-respect, and then your self-worth will shine through. Check in with yourself daily and decide, "Am I taking quality, pristine care of my most important needs?" If you can answer "yes", that will make you feel good *every day*.

You are not wrong for wanting your grandest dreams. They are in your head for a reason. You must open up to embrace your destiny—many people close themselves off after deeming their truest desires impossible. Nothing is impossible. You are here to prove that.

Build a sense of certainty and Know that you are on the right path. Nothing will stand in the way of your goals if you consistently focus on achieving them. You are perfection manifest. This cannot be repeated enough, seeing as you do not yet believe it!

Contentment Within

Aside from taking daily steps towards your most interesting goals, you may discover inner contentment by building your character. As no surprise, first, you must learn to relax at the molecular level. You will know when you reach this state, for you will automatically remember that nothing in this world or beyond can cause you harm, and that fear is simply like a cloud of dust blocking you from your center.

Next, you must develop daily habits which stand by all your foundational character traits—your moral compass. You must complete this work in your daily life. There is no other way to ensure these essential components of character are established and "locked-in," so to speak. Recognizing and then genuinely displaying your integrity and confidence will make you feel content.

Gratitude

It is a sad reality to think that many children who have been raised in the most resource-rich countries in the world do not know what gratitude *feels* like. Do not scoff at such a statement—lack of awareness of gratitude is more detrimental than you can imagine. If a child is not taught to *feel* gratitude with their heart (rather than just thinking about it with their thoughts), that child grows up to be an ungrateful adult without the self-awareness needed to remedy this weakness. You don't know what you don't know—and once you discover this missing piece (that is required to manifest the life you desire), boy, it's a long way to go! This is why teaching children the critical foundations of self-awareness is so vital. Imagine how much progress a generation like that will make.

When you are feeling discouraged or upset about life, have mercy on yourself and count your blessings, so you may remind yourself of all the good you have manifested in your waking reality thus far. The more gratitude you feel within, the more the Truth may pour in. The less gratitude you feel, the more you will close up—and you won't enjoy anything. You won't feel part of this world or of your community.

Gratitude for Small Things

Behold the magnificence of creation right before your eyes. Give thanks for everything around you. Be grateful that you don't have a more extreme example of what to be grateful for. It can take some of the worst situations (rather, what many people would deem "the worst") to develop an extraordinary, well-rooted understanding of gratitude for the simplest things in life—which most people take for granted (a toothbrush or clean water for example).

While pain and suffering occur in dire, poverty-stricken countries, do these people not appreciate life, perhaps more so than many people who live in financially well-off countries? Regardless of where you are, it may be useful to think about this, especially when you find yourself caught in the minutiae of daily living. There is simply no reason to be upset about most things. Save your energy!

To Know vs. To Believe

Here is a useful contemplation tool to further establish your Inner Truth. Examine everything you've learned in your lifetime and determine which things you *Know* and which you *believe*. There is a significant difference between these two concepts, and the explanation below will shed light on why belief systems, in particular, can cause issues.

To say you *Know* something to be true has a different feeling tone, as opposed to saying you *believe* something to be true.

- To *Know* has a sense of awareness, confidence, and depth of wisdom which cannot be shaken easily. True Knowing is

often associated with direct experience and practicality—common sense—knowledge that derives from within and that has been collected straight from Source Itself or your own experience from this life or perhaps another.
- To *believe*, on the other hand, is based on a perception generated outside of oneself. A belief is adopted by someone, perhaps with a bit of laziness, with the *desire* that it is whole and accurate as it has been portrayed by someone else. It does not come from within.

Do you prefer Knowing or believing? Perhaps obviously, true *Knowing* proves far superior to any *belief*, for Knowing comes from your soul, and brings with it depth and self-trust which no person may provide to another. Rather, each individual must Know for themselves. That is the secret to a sound foundation for each person, family, and community at large. Take *responsibility* for your own sense of reality. Do not depend on anyone else to tell you "how things are." You may still learn from others who have accumulated wisdom, but you must take what they say with a grain of salt—or as breadcrumbs to a path you can explore yourself.

So, how does one develop a true Knowing about anything? To develop pristine clarity regarding *any* topic, sit quietly daily, at first with great patience. Listen for the small voice within and you will unlock great secrets the world does not know yet!

Now, what about *global* beliefs—beliefs that have tremendous power over how entire populations conduct their lives, how society is shaped, and even where laws originate? For example, regarding the most ancient spiritual texts, much has been tainted by time, translation, and the betrayal of Truth (for there is a lot of fear in facing Truth, or rather, there is much fear felt by the leaders of this planet that the people will rediscover that their own infinite power resides within, and *not* in the hands of any power-hungry ego-driven madmen).

While we are not here to blame past political or religious leaders or point any fingers, the corruption of the ancient texts that so many people rely on for how to live good, moral lives, is the reason it is *vital* to look within for the answers you seek—all of them. What if the things people are being taught in church are not accurate, or do not penetrate very deeply past mundane thought patterns? What if these religious leaders who hold so much power over their followers are themselves missing the biggest points or spiritual lessons? Do you want to leave such an important part of *your* life up to someone else?

As mentioned above, there is a major difference between believing and Knowing: one originates from outside of you, the other from the inside. When you think about your spiritual path and any knowledge you have been given that you have deemed "accurate and complete," you must determine which is Truth and which is a belief. Does it actually ring through as Truth? Or does it leave you feeling empty, bored, or confused? While churches, governments, schools, and other organizations promote belief systems within entire populations, generation upon generation, we can recognize the disconnect happening here. People have forgotten, and have lost their self-trust, to look within and verify *everything* they've been taught. It is so easy to get distracted by persuasive beliefs, especially when you have no bias or judgments on a topic. So, it becomes easy for someone, with or without an agenda, to swoop in and decide for you, as you will likely ignore the doubts at the back of your mind. That doubtful voice is your intuition, and if you listen to it, it will lead you to Truth.

Do not be fooled by people, especially those with power, who run around thinking they're better than you are. Do not be fooled by religious leaders who claim they can communicate with God better than you. Only you Know. They can only ask you to *believe*. Which do you prefer? Which moves your soul in a meaningful direction, even in the face of adversity, or when risking being called "different" or wrong? If you choose to find Truth, be prepared to face questions from others. If you desire a community of like-minded individuals to help you in your understanding of Truth, we recommend you study with a friend or small group. Find books that speak to your heart (and don't depend *solely* on those which have been translated through multiple languages and edited by kings or others with too much power…).

Truth vs. Perspective

Truth stands alone, of its own accord. Perspective represents the different angles you may view Truth from so that you may get a little closer. Your current perspective is as close to Truth as you have thus far stretched your consciousness, and perspectives from other people may help you further your comprehension.

Human beings are spectators, interpreting Truth from a limited standpoint, using judgment to fill in holes—gaps in awareness—where one does not yet understand a specific topic or another person. It is a better strategy to leave the holes open, so that they may be filled later with a compatible, aligned concept. It is best *not* to fill holes with preconceived judgments or new belief systems, especially where they might be ill-intended, or where they may cause an unnecessary tangle of the brain that will just have to be untangled later, after such a neural network is anchored into the whole ego identity of your worldly Self.

For example, let us say you create a belief about your neighbor that is less than desirable. You interpret what you see them do or say as proof of your newfound label or belief. You decide you don't like them. What you are doing is creating neural networks that continue strengthening as you build your self-made story. When emotions are brought into the picture, then you may also have chemical reactions occur inside your body when you see evidence of your story. Then one day you discover, beyond any doubt, that you were wrong. What happens to these neural networks now? Sometimes people dislike finding out they are wrong and will hold on to their beliefs for as long as they can! It is obviously better to face the truth of any situation, but this requires work, focused brain power, separation from the ego. As you eliminate your beliefs and shift to your newfound truth, you are actively rewiring your brain, which takes energy and a good solid look at the puffed-up ego....

Leadership

Leadership is an important role for everyone to take up, yet most people quickly choose to hand off this responsibility to someone else. Fears of inadequacy are often what cause people to look no further on this great and satisfying path. Truly, each person is already a leader of their own Life, their own Universe, whether they like it or not. So, it is up to each individual to take that responsibility seriously and begin conducting themselves as royal, responsible, courageous leaders *of themselves*. Only then can humanity grow stronger toward a more honorable, self-aware existence in the grander stage of the cosmos.

Once you start doing the work within, others will notice, at least at a subconscious, energetic level. You will appear stronger mentally and emotionally, and also wiser in ways unique to each person you encounter. Some people may fear your power; others will embrace it. Some may loathe it; others may try to take it. They will see your life improving, becoming more in line with your deepest desires and your soul's expansion. Some may be inspired and follow your lead, building up their own lives and becoming the responsible leaders—the Kings and Queens they are destined to be. As for the others, fear not, for they only see in you what they desire to see in themselves. We are, after all, perfect mirrors for each other.

Everyone has their own path, and they must forge it alone. Of course, you may help each other, but each person has an individual path, and it is ultimately up to you to forge yours. To do this requires all the attributes written into Universal Law, however, so you must have courage and commitment to achieve what you desire. Let your passions guide you.

Influencing Others

Tread lightly in others' lives, for you do not know their path, and they do not know yours. You may enjoy intimacy with certain souls, but as with casual friends and acquaintances, you must keep boundaries clear to avoid unsettling disturbances. Do not take it upon yourself to share the wisdom you have discovered if you have not been asked for it directly. Planting seeds is a delicate task, and one that must be executed with precision and a gentle hand. Remember, too, there are only some seasons that are ideal for planting, and only a few seeds are needed at a time...

Plant seeds as gently as you can, without disrupting the environment in which you plant. This is the only way your seed may begin to germinate, unharmed by any defensive barriers that are often put up in another person's mind when seeds are used as weapons of right or wrong and are pelted straight at another person's ego, from your own. Those seeds will never make a dent, and the groundskeepers of someone's mind will be sure to remove them altogether, as foreign unwanted contaminants from an enemy soldier.

If you want your message to be heard, plant a small, friendly seed with no expectations or ulterior motives. Only then will you make progress in truly helping another see, or shift their perspective, in a way that could never have happened otherwise.

Perfection

Many people believe that perfection is an unattainable state or quality—something the human brain defines and considers "the best possible result or condition." But who is to say that the perfection the brain imagines is even possible on the physical plane, especially considering that every single thing is constantly changing on the molecular level, every moment of every day? *This* is the cutting edge of existence, after all. Nothing exists beyond this moment. So by that viewpoint, the state of any creation at this moment is as perfect as it has ever been thus far in this timeline. We could perhaps say that "perfection" in its manifested physical form, changes and evolves with the universe from moment to moment, when we are speaking with regard to time.

Since the beginning, you have been perfect—since the inception of time itself. Do not buy into the belief system that you can never be precisely what you choose to be, which is *perfect* in some form. Seeing yourself grow and *become* the great perfection you imagine is what will give you true satisfaction and enjoyment in this life and beyond—not this feeling of perpetual inadequacy that the perfection of yourself can never be. You are the most perfect version of yourself now, and it would be healthy to appreciate how far you've come.

These sorts of constant changes are inevitable on this forever blossoming physical plane, and yet, there is a layer beneath this which shall forever remain as it is, intact and unchanging. That is the Home we described before. That is where your most creative endeavors derive, always free from fears and your internal egoic protective system. This is where the magic lamp exists within the Cave of Wonders in the story of Aladdin. You must learn to tap this reservoir and perhaps you will achieve immortality. Ahem, this is where the Daily Work comes in handy!

Let us briefly explore this mysterious topic of immortality, for it seems quite unreachable, but is it really? What if Source is the perfect soil and we are its perfect flowers? Some of us maintain excellent access to this perfect soil, while others cut themselves off. Some live long lives and blossom and flourish. Others shrivel up with diseases and wrinkles, and die early. What if we learn to be fully aware of our root system (the world within us) so we can clearly see and heal all blocks and damaged roots (damages from childhood)? Looking at the incomprehensible design of the human body, is there any reason why it would not continually renew so that we could live an immortal life on this planet, as long as we desire to?

17

Glossary

Artificial Matrix: anything outside and things we put into our bodies which negatively impact our naturally pure resonant frequency such as the digital universe, processed foods, radio waves, Wi-Fi, 5G, etc. and all other external noise that clouds our vision of the Kingdom Within (including parasites living in our bodies). Anything that is a step removed from mother nature. The more degrees removed, the more damaging it is.

Daily Work: What you will practice as you go about your daily life. It includes meditation and practicing Universal Law every day. This harmonizes your body, mind, and soul to the Light of Intelligence, Source, [insert your chosen label]. This work begins within, and then you deliver it to your external reality.

Garden of Life, Kingdom Within, Natural Matrix, Heaven, Home: our resting place, where perfect freedom, joy, confidence, self-forgiveness, and unconditional love exist to be fully experienced without striving or a need to earn these gifts of existence. Our real home, where we were born, and where we will return. Picture Aladdin reaching the magic lamp in the Cave of Wonders. Access point: the base of the heart.

The Great Beings Within: a collection of souls and energetic entities who represent my access to Truth. The Source of the information and exercises found in these pages.

Great Teachers: Everyone born onto this planet has an assigned "team," so to speak, that is always here guiding and protecting them along the way. With all the modern-day distractions and toxins, however, most people have lost touch with these guides, which is why civilization has become a bit less lively, disease-ridden, somewhat depressed, and stuck in mediocrity. If you don't know your soul mission, and you would like to, connect with your Great Teachers. This book will help you get there.

Inner Well of Truth and Understanding: the original Source of all inner wisdom. Access point: the base of the heart.

Know, Knowing: heart-centered knowledge derived from within.

know, knowing: intellectually based knowledge; knowledge from the brain.

Life: the grand masterpiece you are living and manifesting from within; your internal reality.

life: the experience of the world around you; your external reality.

Truth: the deep understanding of morals and self-respect each Being is born with. If children are not provided the appropriate environment for their unique growth and expansionary need, as they grow, their access to Truth is clouded and concealed by environmental noise, false beliefs about themselves and reality.

truth: intellectually based facts as we perceive them now.

Oath of Forgiveness: a promise you make to yourself every day to live out your time with grace , gratitude, and respect for yourself. A promise to release all guilt, shame, and emotional baggage, and forgive yourself for all your mistakes and regrets *daily*. A conscious choice to love yourself deeper than you ever have before.

Oneness: Source, God, All That Is, the Light of Intelligence.

Unknown, the Unknowing: an important "blank slate" state to achieve for inner clarity and enlightenment; when one can let go fully of all external knowledge and allow true inner wisdom to flow through at full force, unhindered by preconceived thoughts, "knowledge", beliefs, and insecurities within the brain. Once you arrive in the present moment, this will be your experience.

18

Thank You!

Thank you so much for choosing *Emotional Intelligence Insights for Self Mastery* as part of your self-exploration!

If you found value in this book, I would be honored to have your feedback. A review on Amazon would help me reach more Deep Divers & continue creating content that resonates with you. Your insights are invaluable. **https://www.amazon.com/author/jfinn**

If you have critiques or ideas for the next volume of insights, I'd love to hear them: **info@arkofarion.com**

Thank you for your support—from the bottom of my heart (if you know, you Know ;)